SERVICE CHARGES
2nd edition

Peter Forrester

Acknowledgment

Crown copyright material is reproduced with the permission of the Controller of HMSO and the Queen's Printer for Scotland.

Please note: References to the masculine include, where appropriate, the feminine.

Published by the Royal Institution of Chartered Surveyors (RICS)
Surveyor Court
Westwood Business Park
Coventry CV4 8JE
UK
www.ricsbooks.com

ISBN 978 1 84219 420 1

Typeset in Great Britain by Columns Design Ltd, Reading, Berks

Printed in Great Britain by Page Bros, Milecross Lane, Norwich

Printed on Greencoat Paper – Greencoat is produced using 80% recycled fibre and 20% virgin TCF pulp from sustainable forests.

Contents

Contents

Contents

Contents

Contents

Preface

While chartered surveyors may not need the *breadth* of understanding of the law of their opposite numbers in the legal profession, in a number of key areas of application to property and construction they need a similar *depth* of legal knowledge. Exactly what the key areas may be depends to some extent on the nature of the surveyor's practice; two obvious examples are the law of landlord and tenant and town and country planning. There are plenty of chartered surveyors who know much more about rent reviews or compulsory purchase compensation than the average lawyer in general practice. They need to know the law as much as the valuation principles, not least because the former can affect the latter.

So surveyors require legal knowledge and for a variety of reasons need to develop their understanding of it. Changing trends or individual variations in clients' requirements mean that from time to time even the best practitioners (perhaps especially the best practitioners) will feel the need to expand their knowledge. The knowledge acquired at college or in study for the Assessment of Professional Competence has a limited shelf life and needs to be constantly updated to maintain its currency. Even specialists working in their areas of expertise need a source of reference as an aide-memoire or as a first port of call in more detailed research.

The Case in Point Series

RICS Books is committed to meeting the needs of surveying (and other) professionals and the Case in Point series typifies that commitment. It is aimed at those who need to upgrade or update their legal knowledge, or who need to have access to a good first reference at the outset of an inquiry. A particular difficulty in doing so lies in the area of case law. There are few legal subjects of interest to surveyors where it does not play a role. This is true of areas like landlord and tenant law where, even though a statutory framework exists, interpretation and application of the provisions at the sharp end are provided by judicial decisions. Chartered Surveyors are generally well aware of the importance of case law but are confronted by a significant practical problem in dealing with it, namely, the burgeoning of reported decisions of the courts. The sheer scale of the law reports, both general and specialist, makes it very hard even to be aware of recent trends, let alone identify the significance of a particular decision. Thus it was decided to focus on the developments in case law. In any given matter, the practitioner will want to be directed efficiently to the decision which bears upon the matter with which he or she is dealing; in other words, to the 'case in point'.

The series has developed incrementally since its launch in 2002 and now comprises 15 books covering a wide range of legal subjects relevant to the work of chartered surveyors. In the fields of property investment and management, the key titles are Rent Review, Lease Renewal, Dilapidations, Easements and Party Walls, but there are also pure construction titles such as Construction Claims and Adjudication, as well as those applicable to all disciplines, such as Expert Witness and VAT. The author of each title has the degree of expertise required to be selective and succinct, thus achieving a high level of relevancy without sacrificing accessibility, so that busy practitioners get what they need – the law on the matter they are handling, when they want it.

Service Charges by Peter Forrester

One of the earlier titles commissioned in the series was Service Charges and it is no accident that it is one of the first to appear in a second edition. Nor is it simply a result of commercial success, although it is a fact that the first edition sold several hundred copies within a few months of its release in 2004. The decision to commission a second edition was based on a combination of the importance of the subject and the number of significant developments in the case law. Service charges are notorious for generating friction between landlord and tenant and the last 4 years have seen significant additions to an already ample body of case law.

Peter Forrester, a Director at Savills, with more than 25 years experience in property management, is well-placed to meet one of the principal requirements of a title in the Case in Point series, namely that it must be of direct relevance to practitioners. Not only is he one of the chartered surveyors mentioned at the outset as being well-versed in this specialised area of law, but he can bring to the task an appreciation of the areas which actually give rise to uncertainty and contention in practice – the service charge 'pinch-points'. The author seeks to answer some of the key questions which give rise to conflict, such as whether all costs can be recovered via the service charge and more detailed issues such as the distinction between 'repairs' and improvements. Often he can resolve the matter by reference to the 'case in point', but where factual differences or oddities mean that there is no definitive right answer, there is a least a pointer to judicial attitudes and/or guidance in the commentary.

No text can completely prevent disputes from arising and Peter Forrester would be better aware of this than most, from long experience of commercial property management practice. However, his book will ensure that landlords and tenants and especially their respective professional advisers, approach any issue over service charges properly informed as to what the legal position actually is. The second edition of Service Charges is a landmark in the Case in Point series and a significant contribution to clarification of the case law in this contentious area.

Anthony Lavers, August 2008
Professional Support Lawyer, White & Case, London
Visiting Professor of Law, Oxford Brookes University
Consultant Editor, Case in Point series

Introduction

A lawyer of my acquaintance once described a service charge as a payment by a tenant to his landlord for services that the tenant did not want and could not afford.

Statutory regulation of service charges for residential property was first introduced in the *Housing Finance Act* 1972. Successive legislation, most recently the *Commonhold and Leasehold Reform Act* 2002 has provided residential tenants greater protection against abuse.

There are probably tens of thousands of properties in England and Wales, both residential and commercial, which are the subject of service charge regimes and the majority work perfectly satisfactorily from both sides of the landlord and tenant relationship.

In providing the services the landlord's objective will be to maintain the quality and value of his investment with 100 per cent recovery of the costs incurred, whilst the tenant will seek reasonable enjoyment and use of the premises, at a reasonable cost, excluding unnecessary or inappropriate expenditure or costs that should be borne by the landlord.

Therefore, the aims and expectations of the landlord may often run counter to those of the tenant, which can, on occasion, cause disputes to arise.

The lease is a contract between the landlord and the tenant. The law of contract, the intention of the parties when entering into the contractual arrangement and, in the case of residential dwellings, statutory regulation will therefore govern the service charges provisions.

The precise wording of the clauses of the lease creating the landlord's obligations to provide services to his tenant, and creating his entitlement to the service charge from his tenant, must therefore be considered carefully in order to ascertain the extent of the tenant's liability.

Drafting errors in leases, and grey areas in the interpretation of lease documentation, law and statute will often lead to disputes between the parties, though rarely in practice will the dispute end up in court.

Following the introduction of the *Civil Procedure Rules* (Woolf Reforms) and as surveyors become involved in more detailed landlord and tenant disputes as part of any alternative dispute resolution, it is increasingly important to be conversant with and understand the principles established under case law. As well as helping enhance credibility and the range of arguments put forward in negotiations, the ability to draw on points established in previous cases can help successful settlements to be reached.

For lawyers who may have an extensive knowledge of and be fully up to date on relevant case law, it is equally important to have an understanding of the more practical implications of the many principles established.

Case law can usually be relied upon as establishing rules for later actions but contradictions do occur, often where cases appear to be very similar. The important point to bear in mind therefore, when considering cases as an indication as to how the courts might decide a particular dispute, is that cases often lay down rules on a point of law but that all cases will be decided upon their own particular facts and every case is individual.

The decisions reached by the courts will depend upon the circumstances in each case and the precise interpretation of the documentation, which though apparently similar, may use different wording in an all-important respect.

For instance, a 'cost reasonably incurred' is entirely different to a 'reasonable cost incurred' and a repairing obligation that also contains reference to 'renewal' will create a far greater obligation than an otherwise identical clause that does not.

Care should therefore be taken not to rely upon case law as providing definitive rules on the application of an interpretation of law.

A majority of cases referred to in this book relate to residential tenancies, but the principles established in nearly all cases can generally be taken as applying to both residential and commercial lettings.

This book is not intended as a detailed reference work for the general management and administration of service charges. It is intended to provide a reference to the relevant case law which has established the principles in the light of which service charges are to be managed and administered, in a form that busy professionals can easily assimilate.

Where appropriate, comment is made in relation to any statutory regulation as it affects residential property. Such statutory regulation may reinforce or complement decided cases.

In some cases, statute will supersede earlier case law, but as statute only regulates service charges in respect of residential property, established case law will continue to be relevant to commercial property.

This book is divided into a number of sections. The first deals with the general principles and the contractual basis of the service charges and looks at various key elements of the lease provisions.

The next sections consider what, how and when expenditure is recoverable in respect of matters traditionally considered as true 'services', insurance, repairs, renewals, replacements and improvements.

The topic of repairs, renewals etc. is very complex and many weighty tomes have been published on these subjects. Whilst not intended to be exhaustive, this section does include reference to many cases which are not specifically concerned with service charges. However, particularly in the area of dilapidations, many decisions will have a direct bearing on the type and nature of the expenditure recoverable under a service charge arrangement.

The following sections look at other costs which are often included within the service charge, i.e. sinking and reserve funds, depreciation, management charges and professional fees and the final sections deal with the financial administration of the service charge including funding, on-account payments and estimates, apportionments and certification.

List of Acts and abbreviations

The following Acts are referenced in this publication. Where an Act is mentioned frequently, it is referred to by the abbreviation that follows the name of the Act in brackets.

Commonhold and Leasehold Reform Act 2002 (**'CLRA 2002'**)

Companies Act 1985

Companies Act 1989

Disability Discrimination Act 1995

Landlord and Tenant Act 1954

Landlord and Tenant Act 1985 (**'LTA 1985'**)

Landlord and Tenant Act 1987 (**'LTA 1987'**)

Local Government Planning and Land Act 1980

Health and Safety at Work Act 1974

Housing Act 1961

Housing Act 1980

Housing Act 1996

Housing Finance Act 1972

Service Charges (Consultation Requirements) (England) Regulations 2003 (SI 2003/1987)

Supply of Goods and Services Act 1982

Theft Act 1968

The text of this publication is divided into commentary and case summaries. The commentary is enclosed between grey highlighted lines for ease of reference.

Table of cases

1
General principles

A service charge is the mechanism by which the landlord recovers from tenants that expenditure which the landlord expends in relation to the repair and maintenance of the building, plant and machinery and the provision of services.

Section 18 of the *Landlord and Tenant Act* 1985 ('LTA 1985') defines a service charge as:

> 'An amount payable by a tenant of a dwelling as part of or in addition to the rent–
>
> (a) which is payable directly or indirectly for services, repairs, maintenance or insurance or the landlord's cost of management, and
>
> (b) the whole or part of which varies or may vary according to the relevant costs.'

The *Commonhold and Leasehold Reform Act* 2002 ('CLRA 2002') amended this definition to amounts payable by the tenant for 'services, repairs, maintenance, improvements, or insurance or the landlord's cost of management'.

The fundamental distinction between residential and commercial service charges has been the introduction of statutory regulation in the residential sector, which provides protection for tenants against abuse. The commercial sector has no such statutory regulation or control.

The legal framework applying to service charges comprise three principle sources:

(1) the contract;

(2) statutory regulation; and

(3) case law.

The extent to which the landlord will be obliged to provide and carry out works and services will, in respect of both commercial and residential leases, depend upon the strict interpretation of the wording of the lease. LTA 1985, subsequently amended by the *Housing Act* 1996 and CLRA 2002, imposes statutory constraints in respect of service charges for residential properties.

However, the recent cases of *Heron Maple House Ltd v Central Estates* (2002) and *Oakfern Properties Ltd v Ruddy* (2006) have determined that a landlord of a lease that includes both residential and non-residential elements will also need to follow the statutory procedures laid by LTA 1985 (as amended) to ensure that non-recovery does not result due to an infringement of the legislation designed to protect residential occupants only.

Where the lease contains both residential and commercial premises the commercial service charge would in effect no longer be governed solely by the law of contract but could also benefit from the statutory regulation usually only afforded to residential tenants.

1.1 WHEN IS A SERVICE CHARGE PAYABLE?

1.1.1 Contractual liability

A tenant will only be liable for payment of a service charge so far as the lease provides for one.

A landlord's obligations to provide services and a tenant's covenant to reimburse a proportion of the cost of the service will depend almost exclusively upon the wording of the lease.

In the absence of any wording, neither a tenant nor a landlord can insist upon including a service charge provision even though the landlord undertook obligations relating to the supply of services.

Riverlate Properties Ltd v Paul (1974)

The tenant covenanted to pay one half of the costs of insurance, exterior decoration and water rates. The same paragraph in the lease provided that the landlord was responsible for exterior and structural repairs. The lease therefore contained no provision for the tenant to bear any costs relating to exterior or structural repairs.

The landlord sought rectification of the lease and it was held:

(1) that since the tenant neither directly not indirectly knew of the landlord's mistake, and since the tenant was not guilty of sharp practice, there was no justification for rectification either on the ground of a common mistake or on the ground of knowledge on the tenant's side that the landlord was making a mistake at the time the lease was granted; and

(2) that where there was a unilateral mistake by the lessor, there was no principle of law which entitled the lessor to rescind or annul the agreement or to require the lessee, who had acquired an interest on the terms on which he had intended to obtain it, to accede to the terms which the lessor meant to impose but did not.

1.1.2 An assumption that the contract is complete

Where there is a contract governing the arrangements between the parties, the courts will usually assume it is complete and will only allow it to be supplemented by other documents in exceptional circumstances.

Universities Superannuation Scheme Ltd v Marks and Spencer plc (1998)

Mummery LJ said:

'The purpose of the service charge provisions is relevant to the meaning and effect. So far as the scheme, context and language of those provisions allow, the service charge provisions should be given an effect that fulfils rather than defeats their evident purpose. The service charge provisions have a clear purpose: the landlord that reasonably incurs liability for expenditure in maintaining ... (the property) ... for the benefit of all its tenants should be entitled to recover the full cost of doing so from those tenants and each tenant should reimburse the landlord a proper proportion of those services charges.'

1.1.3 There is no presumption that the landlord is able to effect full recovery of all costs incurred

If the landlord covenants to provide works or services, he may not have the ability to recover the costs incurred unless clear wording has been included within the service charge provisions enabling him to do so.

The existence of a service charge provision in itself will not always mean that all expenditure incurred by the landlord is necessarily recoverable. There is usually no presumption that the service charge provisions of the lease will automatically entitle the landlord to recover all expenditure.

Based on the contra preferentum rule, the courts will generally favour the tenant when interpreting any ambiguity and where the arguments are evenly matched.

Riverlate Properties Ltd v Paul (1974)

The landlord was responsible for exterior and structural repairs. The tenant covenanted to pay one half of the costs of insurance, exterior decoration and water rates. It was held that the lease therefore contained no provision for the tenant to bear any costs relating to exterior or structural repairs.

Boldmark v Cohen (1986)

A tenant was liable to pay a percentage of costs, expenses and outgoings incurred in carrying out maintenance of a block of flats. The lease included for payments of such other sums as the lessor may from time to time expend in respect of the general administration and management of the block. The landlord sought to recover interest on money borrowed in order to carry out maintenance or provide services in accordance with the contractual obligations. The Court of Appeal held that, although in some circumstances, express provision in a lease enabling tenants to be charged interest might be sensible, the lease in this case did not provide for reimbursement of interest by clear and unambiguous words and therefore the lease, on proper construction, was not capable of including interest payments.

Lloyds Bank plc v Bowker Orford (1992)

The tenant covenanted to pay a service charge being the due proportion of the total cost to the lessor of providing, amongst other things, a lift service, a caretaker, security, cleaning and lighting of common parts, cleaning and lighting of lavatories, constant hot water, and 'any other beneficial services which may properly be provided by the lessee'.

There was a specific landlord's covenant to repair the outside of the building but no reference to repairs in the list of services for which the landlord was entitled to recover.

The landlord sought to recover the costs of external repairs and internal decoration and repairs of the common parts of the building.

It was held that a proportion of the cost of external repairs and internal decorations and repairs of the common parts were not recoverable as not being 'beneficial services'.

The landlord was under an obligation to carry out external repairs and if it had intended to recover the costs it would have been very simple to reserve the right by reference to it in the list of service charges.

Therefore, if the landlord has in mind the provision of a service, but he has not covered the right to include the cost of providing it in the service charge, he will not generally be able to argue that he has the power to provide the service under the sweeper clause, and to recover the cost.

Broadwater Court Management Company Ltd v Jackson-Mann (1997)

Service charge provisions in respect of leases of a block of flats did not expressly include costs relating to annual auditing and filing of statutory returns under the *Companies Act* 1989. A company established by the tenants to acquire the freehold of the block sought to recover such costs within the service charge but were prevented from doing so as the leases made no specific provision for the recovery of such costs, which were not intended at the time the leases were granted.

1.1.4 Because a particular expense can be reimbursed by way of the service charge does not mean that it must be

Shah v Colvia Management Company Ltd (2008)

This case involved a large industrial estate which was managed by a tenant-owned management company. On-site car parking spaces were not demised or allocated to tenants under the terms of the long leases although each tenant had the right to use the car parking spaces subject to reasonable management regulations.

The on-site parking provision was insufficient, the problem being exacerbated because several tenants, principally vehicle repairers, also left vehicles in the spaces overnight. The local authority issued a rates demand in respect of the car parks which the landlord sought to recover through the service charge.

However, this was resisted by a majority of tenants who had difficulties in parking. The management company sought to introduce a charging system for overnight parking with the income generated being set against the rates demand.

This proposal was resisted by the vehicle repairers on the basis that as a result of the charges, they would in effect be paying the entire rates demand, which was an expense which should be shared by all tenants via the service charge.

The Court of Appeal overturned the earlier High Court decision and held that the burden of proof lay with the vehicle repairers to show the scheme was unreasonable. The Court also commented that it was not unreasonable in principle that those who benefit from a service should pay for the privilege, even though this had the result that expenditure, which would otherwise be recovered by way of the service charge, is met in a different way.

1.1.5 Rectification of defective wording

Where it appears that the intention of the lease is to give the landlord the right to include a particular service, but the wording of the lease is defective, the courts will rectify the lease or so interpret it as to a make sense of what is apparently intended.

Edmonton Corporation v WM Knowles & Son Ltd (1961)

A tenant of factory premises covenanted to pay to the landlord 'the cost (as certified by the borough architect for the time being) of painting in a workmanlike manner every third year of the term all outside wood and metal work and other external parts of the demised premises'. However, the landlord had not expressly reserved a right of entry although it did in respect of other terms in the lease.

It was held that having regard to the tenant's express obligation to reimburse the landlord the cost of redecorations, there was an implied obligation on the landlord to paint the premises and, of necessity, a licence to enter the premises to carry out the works must also be implied.

Skilleter and others v Charles (1992)

The Court held that the landlord was able to recover interest on borrowed money. Notwithstanding that some words had been omitted in the relevant clause, the plain intention was that interest should be chargeable and to give effect to the intention it was only necessary to insert the obviously missing words or that the same could be achieved by implying a term that interest should be payable in order to give business efficacy to the terms of the lease.

1.1.6 Landlord's obligations to provide services

In the absence of specific wording, the inclusion of an item within a service charge provision does not place an obligation on the landlord to provide that service.

Russel v Laimond Properties Ltd (1984)

Under the lease, the landlord could recover the cost of providing porterage services including the cost of providing, maintaining and repairing a porter's flat. It was held that the fact the landlord could recover such costs did not impose an obligation upon the landlord to provide a resident porter.

Jacey Property Co Ltd v de Sousa (2003)

The Court refused to impose an obligation on the landlord to carry out repairs to drains, even though the lease entitled him to recover these costs as part of the service charge.

1.1.7 Implied obligation to provide services

An obligation to provide services in particular circumstances may be implied in order to give business efficacy to an arrangement.

Liverpool City Council v Irwin (1976)

The Court implied into a tenancy of a council flat in a tower block, an obligation on the landlord to keep the common parts, lifts and rubbish chutes in repair and properly lighted. In this case, the landlord retained occupation of the essential means of access to units in the building with no obligation attaching to those units to maintain the access.

Barrett v Lounova (1982) Ltd (1989)

A tenant covenanted to keep the inside of the premises in good repair. The agreement was silent in respect of the liability for keeping the outside of the premises in good repair. In order to give business efficacy to the agreement, the landlord was held to have an implied obligation to maintain the exterior of a house where the tenant had covenanted to maintain the interior.

1.1.8 Limitation to implied obligations

Where a lease contains detailed provisions, the scope for the implication of terms will be severely limited.

Duke of Westminster v Guild (1983)

A tenant's lease contained an express grant of a right of way over the landlord's retained property to the public highway. The tenant covenanted to pay a fair proportion of the expenses of making, repairing and scouring walls, drains, etc. A drain serving the premises was defective and the tenant argued that, in the absence of an express covenant, the lease imposed an implied contractual obligation on the landlord to keep in repair and unobstructed the landlord's part of the drain. Alternatively, the landlord was under a duty of care to keep the drain in repair.

It was held that the normal test for an implied term of necessity in order to give efficacy to the lease was not satisfied in this case and, furthermore, the landlord was not under a duty of care to repair a drain through which the tenant had an easement.

Hafton Properties Ltd v Camp (1994)

The tenant covenanted with the lessor and the management company, incorporated to manage the building and provide services, to pay a maintenance charge being a specific proportion of the management company's costs expended in respect of certain items. The management company covenanted to carry out repairs and maintenance.

It was held that a term could not be implied that the lessor would observe the covenants for repair and maintenance on behalf of the management company. The more comprehensive a code in the lease (for the carrying out of repairs and the payment of them) the less room there is for the implication of a term.

1.2   ARE ALL COSTS RECOVERABLE?

Section 18 of LTA 1985 defines a service charge as:

'An amount payable by a tenant as part or in addition to the rent either directly or indirectly for services, repairs, maintenance or insurance or the landlord's costs of management, the whole or part of which varies or may vary according to the relevant costs.'

For commercial property, the basic principle, in the absence of any statutory definition, is that where a service charge operates, a tenant should expect to pay, and the landlord should expect to be reimbursed, all costs legitimately spent on a property and which, in other circumstances, one would expect to be spent by an owner-occupier or would be expected of, and enforced upon, a tenant occupying on full repairing and insuring terms.

1.2.1 Assumption that items not listed are not recoverable

Even under a lease that contains a detailed service charge clause, there may be landlord's expenditure that falls outside the wording of the clause and would not then be recoverable from the tenant. There is no presumption that service charge provisions are automatically intended to enable a landlord to recover all his costs for the provision of services.

Based on the *expressio unius est exclusio alterius* rule, where a list of items is inserted, there is an assumption that items not on the list are not to be charged.

Rapid Results College v Angell (1986)

Tenants of premises comprising the top floor of a building were required to contribute towards the maintenance of the exterior of the first and second floor offices and repairs and maintenance of all other parts of the building used in common with the landlords and tenants and occupiers of other portions of the building. The parapet of the building had to be rebuilt after the bricks became saturated with damp.

It was held that, in the context of the lease, the roof could not be regarded as part of the exterior of the offices and the landlord could not recover the costs of repairs, even though the tenant benefited from the repairs. The Court also rejected a claim that the costs were recoverable as repairs and maintenance in respect of parts of the building used 'in common' by the landlord and tenants of other portions of the building.

Sella House Ltd v Mears (1989)

A lease entitled the landlord to recover 'fees of agents or other persons managing the building including the cost of computing and collecting rents and service charges' and the cost of 'employing professional persons necessary or desirable for the proper maintenance, safety and administration of the building'. It was held that the landlord was not able to recover the costs of lawyer's fees incurred in recovering rent and service charges.

1.2.2 The costs of statutory compliance

If the landlord incurs costs as a result of compliance with statute, but the lease does not provide for the recovery of such costs, the landlord will not be able to recover his expenditure even though it was as a result of a legal requirement.

Broadwater Court Management Company Ltd v Jackson-Mann (1997)

Service charge provisions in respect of leases of a block of flats did not expressly include costs relating to annual auditing and filing of statutory returns under the *Companies Act* 1985. A company established by the tenants to acquire the freehold of the block sought to recover such costs within the service charge but were prevented from doing so as the leases made no specific provision and the recovery of such costs were not intended at the time the leases were granted.

1.2.3 Statement that landlord is to be indemnified against all costs and expenses

Where a lease states that the landlord is to be indemnified against all costs and expenses, or entitles the landlord to recover the 'total costs' of works or services, this may widen the scope of items recoverable under the service charge.

Lloyds Bank plc v Bowker Orford (1992)

The landlord sought to recover the costs of capital as opposed to revenue expenditure in respect of plant and equipment providing hot water to the lavatories, the heating of the common parts and the provision of lifts. It was held that the specified services recoverable under the lease were not limited to revenue items and the landlord was entitled to recover the 'total cost' of providing the services.

Daejan Properties Ltd v Bloom (2000)

The tenant of a basement garage, located beneath a courtyard serving a block of 109 flats, covenanted to pay a reasonable proportion of the charges for rebuilding, repairing and cleansing all walls, fences, drains and other 'conveniences' belonging to the premises and capable of being used by the lessee in common with the owners or occupiers of adjoining or contiguous premises.

It was held that the tenant was responsible for the cost of works to replace the asphalt membrane to the concrete slab, which comprised the roof of the garage premises and on which the forecourt and the flats were built, as this was a 'convenience' within the meaning of the lease.

However, it was also held that if it were to be established that works carried out by the lessor over the years had damaged the asphalt membrane, that the proportion of the damage should not be the responsibility of anyone other than the landlord. Conversely, in so far as any part of the damage to the membrane had been caused by incorrect laying in the first instance or wear and tear over the years, this would fall under the repairing covenant for which the lessee was responsible.

1.3 THE SERVICE CHARGE PROVISIONS MUST BE CLEAR AND UNAMBIGUOUS

Where there is a contract governing the arrangements between the parties, the courts will usually assume it is complete and will only allow it to be supplemented by other documents in exceptional circumstances.

Based upon the contra preferentum rule, the courts will generally favour the tenant when interpreting any ambiguity and where the arguments are evenly matched.

1.3.1 For the avoidance of doubt, the lease should clearly state any costs that are to be excluded

Where a tenant does not believe it should contribute towards those parts of the building or in respect of services it cannot enjoy, the lease should be clear on the point.

Broomleigh Housing Association v Hughes (1999)

A tenant in a block of flats covenanted to contribute proportionately to the service charge.

The landlord covenanted to keep the property in good repair. The landlord replaced windows in other flats, but not those in the tenant's flat as these had been recently replaced at the tenant's own expense.

Notwithstanding that the replacement of the windows in the tenant's flat did not constitute a breach of covenant as the landlord has subsequently given the requisite consent, it was held that this did not reduce or vary the obligation upon the tenant to contribute to the total service charge. There was no provision in the lease to allow for this to happen.

Furthermore, the fact that the landlord might have waived the obligation to contribute for some tenants, that is to say those who had obtained a prior written consent, does not create any right or expectation that other tenants should be treated in the same way provided the waiver did not increase the liability of other tenants and any loss arising from such a waiver falls upon the landlord.

Billson and others v Tristrem (2000)

A tenant of a basement flat of a property divided into five flats covenanted to pay 20 per cent of the proportion of the costs of maintaining entrances, passages, landings and staircases 'enjoyed or used by the lessee in common'. The tenant was held to be liable for payment of a proportion of the costs of maintaining the main entrance even though access to the basement flat was by way of separate entrance and the tenant did not have the right to use the main entrance. In this case, whilst the wording of the lease was inappropriate, it was no coincidence that the percentage was specified as 20 per cent per flat.

1.3.2 Additional wording may widen the scope of recoverable costs

The detailed wording of the service charge clause needs to be carefully considered as additional wording may widen the scope of works for which a tenant may be responsible.

Daejan Properties Ltd v Bloom (2000)

The tenant of a basement garage, located beneath a courtyard serving a block of 109 flats, covenanted to pay a reasonable proportion of the charges for rebuilding, repairing and cleansing all walls, fences, drains and other 'conveniences' belonging to the premises and capable of being used by the lessee in common with the owners or occupiers of adjoining or contiguous premises.

It was held that the tenant was responsible for the cost of the works to replace the asphalt membrane to the concrete slab, which comprised the roof of the garage premises and on which the forecourt and the flats were built, as this was a 'convenience' within the meaning of the lease.

1.4 THE LANDLORD SHOULD NOT MAKE A PROFIT FROM THE PROVISION OF THE SERVICES

The basic principle is that the landlord should seek to recover only the costs of providing the various works and services that are recoverable under the service charge provisions of the lease and it is not intended that the landlord should profit from the provision of the services.

Jollybird Ltd v Fairzone Ltd (1990)

The landlord covenanted to repair and maintain a central heating system. The tenants covenanted to pay a fair proportion of the expenses incurred, calculated by reference to floor area, such charge being not less than a fixed rate per square foot and which could be 'increased proportionately at any time ... if the cost of fuel ... shall at any time exceed the cost thereof at the date of the lease'.

The landlord sought to increase the rate per square foot stated in the lease based on the percentage increase in fuel costs which would have resulted in the landlord making a profit from the supply of heating. It was held that the landlord was only entitled to make a charge calculated by reference to floor area, subject to the minimum charge set out in the lease. Although a profit might arise where fuel costs were below the minimum charge, the proviso could not be construed as intending to give the landlord a profit in other circumstances.

1.5 DO COSTS HAVE TO BE REASONABLE?

Supply of Goods and Services Act 1982, s. 13

In a contract for the supply of a service where the supplier is acting in the course of a business, there is an implied term that the supplier will carry out the service with reasonable care and skill.

Landlord and Tenant Act 1985

For residential dwellings, where s. 18 of LTA 1985 applies, s. 19 provides that:

(a) costs can only be recovered if they are reasonably incurred; and

(b) only works or services performed to a reasonable standard can be charged.

Commonhold and Leasehold Reform Act 2002

Section 155 introduced a new s. 27A to LTA 1985 and came into force on 30 September 2003. This provision gives leaseholders and landlords the right to ask a leasehold valuation tribunal (LVT) to determine the reasonableness of a service charge, and also the liability to pay the charge. An application can be made whether or not any payment has been made by the tenant, and a matter is not to be taken as agreed or admitted by virtue of a person having paid all or part of the sum in question.

1.5.1 There is a distinction between reasonable costs and costs reasonably incurred

Forcelux Ltd v Sweetman (2001)

The landlord incurred expenditure on insurance, maintenance and management fees which it sought to recover as service charge items. The tenants referred the charges to the LVT under s. 19(2A) of LTA 1985. On appeal the Lands Tribunal held that s. 19(2A) was not concerned with whether costs were 'reasonable' but whether they were 'reasonably incurred'.

On the question of insurance, whilst the tenants were penalised because cover for commercial landlords was more expensive than that available to owner-occupiers, it was for the landlord to insure and this was not an option for the tenants. The landlord's block policy had been competitively obtained in accordance with market rates and accordingly the costs of insurance premiums were reasonably incurred.

As to the maintenance costs, it was established that the sums involved were in excess of an appropriate market rate. It was therefore held that the tenants should not be saddled with a cost that appears from the evidence to be substantially in excess of what could be reasonably be construed as a market rate.

And on the subject of management fees generally, these were held to be in line with rates charged by local managing agents. The charges made were not excessive and therefore reasonably incurred.

1.5.2 An increase in the cost of repairs resulting from the landlord's failure to attend to disrepair in a timely manner would not be costs 'reasonably incurred'

Continental Property Ventures Inc v White and another (2006)

Leases in respect of a block of flats contained provision for recovery of service charges in respect of expenditure by the landlord on, amongst other things, repairs.

The issue before the Lands Tribunal was an appeal against an earlier LVT decision as to whether a number of items of service charge expenditure had been 'reasonably incurred' within the meaning of s. 19(1)(a) of LTA 1985.

It was held: (i) that the cost of damp-proofing works on the ground floor were disallowed as they should have been carried out at no charge under a guarantee; and (ii) only £3,525 of repairs to one of the flats, carried out at a cost of

£17,114 had been reasonably incurred as a result of the landlords neglect in repairing a leaking pipe.

1.5.3   Implication not to be unreasonable

In respect of commercial properties, the absence of any specific reference in the lease as to whether the costs or the supply of services should be reasonable, there is an implied term that, when spending the tenants' money, the landlord has an obligation not to be unreasonable.

Finchbourne v Rodrigues (1976)

It was held that the parties to the lease could not have intended the landlord to have absolute discretion to accept the highest conceivable sums for maintenance and recover the cost incurred. Therefore, in order to give business efficacy to the lease, a term was to be implied into the lease that the costs recovered should be 'fair and reasonable'.

Firstcross Ltd v Teasdale (1983)

A rent officer or rent assessment committee considering whether or not to register a rent as variable in accordance with the terms governing service charges is confined to an examination of the reasonableness of the terms of variation themselves, having regard: (i) first to the contract between the parties; and (ii) to the terms implied by case law (*Finchbourne v Rodrigues*) and by statute (*Housing Act* 1980), that such charges are only recoverable to the extent that they are fair and reasonable, reasonably incurred and to a reasonable standard.

Morgan v Stainer (1993)

Tenants were required to contribute to a specified sum for the carrying out of maintenance. Under para. 5(b) of the standard form of lease, the tenants were also obliged 'to pay all legal and other costs that may be incurred by the landlord in obtaining the payment of the maintenance contribution from any tenant in the building'.

Some years prior, the tenants had issued proceedings against the landlord on a related matter, which were settled on terms including that the landlord paid the tenants' costs. The landlord then sought to recover the cost incurred in relation to the earlier proceedings under para. 5(b).

It was held that the costs were not 'costs incurred in obtaining the payment of the maintenance contribution' but costs incurred in resisting the tenants' proceedings. The agreement reached was also clear that the landlord was to pay the tenants' costs and the tenants could not then be liable to pay through another route.

Moreover, applying established principles the 'legal and other costs' had to be reasonably and properly incurred, not only with regard to their amount but also with regard to their nature. As the landlord had agreed to pay the tenants' costs, there had to be a presumption that the sums claimed were not reasonable or properly incurred.

1.5.4 Costs should not be exorbitant

Where there is no express or implied duty to be reasonable, the landlord is not obliged to obtain competitive estimates or accept the cheapest quote although there is an implication that costs must not be exorbitant.

Bandar Property Holdings v JS Darwen (Successors) Ltd (1968)

A landlord covenanted to insure premises against specified risks 'in some insurance office of repute'. The tenants obtained a lesser quote for identical insurance to that effected by the landlord. The Court held that a term obliging the landlord to place the insurance so as not to impose an unnecessarily heavy burden on the tenants could not be implied.

Havenridge Ltd v Boston Dyers (1994)

A lease obliged tenants to pay sums that the landlord shall 'properly expend or pay to any insurance company in respect of ... insuring ... the demised premises'. The Court held that 'properly' meant legitimately and that it was neither necessary nor clearly intended that there should be an implication of reasonableness. Provided the insurance was effected in accordance with the terms of the lease (i.e. placed with an insurer 'of repute'), the contract was negotiated at arm's length and the rate was representative of the market value, the landlord was not obliged to seek alternative cheaper quotes.

Berrycroft Management Co Ltd v Sinclair Gardens Investments (Kensington) Ltd (1997)

Leases of a block of flats imposed a requirement on the management company to insure the building for such sums and through such companies as the landlord may direct. The lessees covenanted to pay an appropriate proportion of the insurance cost. It was held that there was no implied covenant that the sum charged by the insurers should be reasonable or that a tenant should not be required to pay a substantially higher sum than he could himself arrange. It was also found that the amounts charged were neither unreasonable nor excessive and were in line with market rates.

1.5.5 The length of the lease may determine what is reasonable

Irrespective of any reference made in the lease as to whether the cost or supply of services or works should be reasonable, the length of the original or unexpired term of the tenant's lease is a factor in deciding if costs are recoverable.

Scottish Mutual Assurance plc v Jardine Public Relations Ltd (1999)

The tenant occupied part of the second floor of an office block under a three-year lease. The landlord carried out only short-term repairs to the roof, intended to deal with immediate leakage problems. The landlord then carried out more extensive repair work and sought recovery of a proportion of the costs from the tenant.

The Court ruled that the tenant was only liable to pay a proportion of the service charge demanded. Whilst accepted as repairs and not improvements, the landlord was only entitled to recover the costs of complying with its repairing obligation over the period of the lease and not more extensive works carried out in performance of the landlord's obligations over a longer term. The fact that the lease was close to expiry was a contributing factor.

Fluor Daniel Properties Ltd and others v Shortlands Investments Ltd (2001)

Leases of a modern commercial block required the landlord to maintain equipment and to provide air-conditioning and other services. The air-conditioning system was well maintained and in good working order. The landlord sought to recover £2m under the service charge provisions for upgrading the system. The landlord sought to rely on the wording of the repairing covenant, which gave the landlord express power to make reasonable additions and variations to the services.

On the question of reasonableness, it was held that the standard had to be such as the tenants, given the lengths of their lease, could fairly be expected to pay for and the landlord could not reasonably overlook the relatively limited interest of the paying tenants. If the landlord wished to carry out repairs which go beyond those which the tenants, given their more limited interest, can be fairly expected to pay, then, subject always to the terms of the lease, the landlord must bear the additional costs himself.

Note: Both the above cases do not give tenants the authority that, as a general rule, they cannot be required to pay a higher service charge for works carried out towards the end of the term. If a landlord can demonstrate that repairs are necessary to comply with its obligations under the terms of the lease and within the life of the lease, the costs are likely to be recoverable even from a tenant whose lease is about to end.

1.5.6 Landlord's discretion as to how services are performed

A landlord, acting reasonably, may be able to recover costs of permanent repairs even though cheaper alternative works could have been carried out.

If a covenant can be performed in more ways than one, it is for the party who covenants to perform the service or carry out the works, acting reasonably, to choose the manner of performance and the discharge of the obligations made under the lease.

Manor House Drive Ltd v Shahbazian (1965)

A landlord covenanted to 'maintain, repair and decorate the main structure and roof of the building'. A leak occurred in the roof and the landlord's surveyor recommended replacement of the roof covering. The tenants claimed that a cheaper, less permanent repair could have been carried out. It was held that the works undertaken were a reasonable and proper way of maintaining the roof. Even though a permanent repair would not make a great financial saving, even in the long term, the landlord was entitled to undertake repairs that were reasonable and proper.

Murray v Birmingham City Council (1987)

There was an implied covenant under s. 32 of the Housing Act 1961 (now replaced by s. 11–16 of LTA 1985) for the landlord to carry out repairs to the roof. The landlord had carried out periodic repairs over time. It was held that the roof was capable of being repaired by periodic attention and had not yet reached the stage when the only practical remedial action was replacement of the roof as a whole.

Reston Ltd v Hudson (1990)

Timber window frames were found to be defective and it was more satisfactory and cheaper to replace all the timber windows at the same time than to leave it to individual tenants to do so from time to time. An issue arose as to the responsibility for replacement and whether the cost would be covered by the service charge.

The lessor covenanted to repair the windows and structures of the estate other than those for which the lessees were responsible. The service charge payable included 'cost and expenses incurred by the lessor' including the matters for which the lessor was responsible under the repairing covenants.

The lessor sought first to inform the tenants of the proposals and, having received certain objections from some tenants, took the precaution of going to the Court for an appropriate declaration.

It was held that the replacing of the windows would be properly recoverable under the service charge.

Postel Properties Ltd v Boots the Chemist Ltd (1996)

The landlords carried out repairs to low-level roofs and upper windows of a large shopping centre. The flat low-level roofs, which were constructed in 1975 and 1976 with a maximum life expectancy of 20 years, were re-covered under a phased programme. The tenants argued that the replacement of the roof covering was premature and the specification was increased to a point where there was an irrecoverable excess, and that the work to the windows was due to rust which could have been contained with timeous maintenance.

It was held that the repairs to the roof were repairs that a reasonably minded building owner might undertake and they did not amount to giving back to the landlord something different from that which existed before. It was reasonable to commence them when the landlord did, notwithstanding that some parts had not yet failed. The works to the windows and cladding were repairs, and, in so far as the landlord may have been guilty of delay in carrying out such works, that was more than balanced by the saved costs of earlier repainting.

Wandsworth London Borough Council v Griffin (2000)

A block of flats were constructed with flat roofs and had metal-framed windows which were in disrepair. Wandsworth London Borough Council replaced the flat roofs with pitched roofs and the windows with uPVC double-glazed units. It was held that within the meaning of the Council's repairing obligations, the works constituted repair as they were cheaper than the alternatives, taking into account both initial and future costs and that the decision to replace the flat roofs with pitched roofs, and the windows with uPVC double-glazed units, was a reasonable one.

1.5.7 Limitation of choice

A tenant's ability to choose the mode of performance of a covenant will be severely limited if the covenant is to be performed 'to the landlord's satisfaction'.

Mason v TotalFinaElf (2003)

The tenant covenanted that it would 'to the satisfaction of the Lessor's Surveyor well and substantially uphold support maintain amend repair decorate and keep in good condition the demised premises'. The landlord brought a claim for dilapidations and it was held that reference to the works being 'to the satisfaction of the Landlord's Surveyor' entitled the landlord's surveyor to prescribe what works should be done and the manner in which the work was to be performed. However, it did not give the landlord's surveyor carte blanche to determine what was required and, if acting reasonably, the surveyor came to a decision that a reasonable surveyor could reach, it would not matter if the tenant would prefer a cheaper, but no less reasonable, option.

1.5.8 Where a lease is clear and unambiguous, the terms must be applied even if unfairness results

The courts will usually have no alternative but to follow a lease even if the proper interpretation of the lease gives rise to an unfair or unjust result. If the lease sets down clear and unambiguous conditions, for example a requirement for prior consultation with tenants prior to incurring expenditure, the landlord would be unable to recover the expenditure even though the tenants were aware of the landlord's intention to incur costs.

CIN Properties Ltd v Barclays Bank plc (1986)

An agreement obliged the tenant to pay a proportion of the costs of repairs subject to the proviso that the landlord would not accept any estimates or place orders for work without first submitting them to the tenant for approval. The landlord placed orders for the carrying out of extensive works without consulting the tenant. The Court of Appeal held that the proviso was an unequivocal condition precedent to the tenant's liability.

Northways Flats Management Co (Camden) v Wimpey Pension Trustees (1992)

The tenant of ground floor commercial premises covenanted to pay a service charge in respect of works of repair. The lease provided that in respect of major works the landlord was to submit a copy of the specification of works and estimates obtained to the tenant for consideration and in the event that the tenant did not raise objections within 21 days, the tenant shall be deemed to have accepted the specification and estimates as reasonable. It was held that the costs of works carried out were not recoverable as there was a specific obligation upon the landlord that was an essential part of the mechanism for the resolution of disputes.

1.5.9   Overcharging – a criminal offence?

There is a possibility that overcharging of a service charge can, if it is grossly excessive, amounts to an offence under s. 15 of the *Theft Act* 1968.

> 'If a tradesman quoted excessively highly for work or services, he would not inevitably come into contact with the criminal law. But if there was a false representation that the amount was fair and reasonable, then there would be a strong possibility of criminality being involved. The fact that no pressure was given to accept a quotation would not avoid criminal liability.'

Lord Justice Watkins in *R v Silverman*

1.6   IS BENEFIT NECESSARY?

1.6.1   A tenant could be liable for the cost of services for which he receives no benefit

Particularly in mixed-use buildings, one tenant or a group of tenants might benefit disproportionately from works and services provided by the landlord. However, where a lease provides for the tenant to contribute a fixed percentage towards the cost incurred by the landlord, the tenant may be liable for a proportion of the cost of a chargeable item even though he does not receive any direct benefit.

Twyman v Charrington (1994)

The tenant of the ground floor and basement of a dwelling house comprising basement to second floors covenanted to contribute and pay a rateable or due proportion of the cost and expenses expended by the landlord in repairing, maintaining, renewing and rebuilding, amongst other things, mutual or party walls and fences, mutual or party structures and other items which may belong to or be used for the demised premises in common with other premises near or adjacent thereto.

The landlord incurred expenditure in repairing the roof and it was held that the fact that the roof was not physically adjacent to the demised premises did not prevent it being regarded as a 'mutual structure' or that, alternatively, the roof fell within the definition of 'other items'.

Thamesmead Town Ltd v Allotey (1998)

The rights of tenants enjoying a right to buy properties on a former GLC housing estate were preserved and the freehold transferred to the secure tenants who entered into covenants 'to the intent that this covenant shall bind the property into whosoever hands the same may come, for the benefit of … Thamesmead' to observe and perform certain restrictions and covenants. The transfer granted no rights over landscaped and communal areas. A dispute arose over an invoice for a provisional service charge requiring the payment of a fair proportion of all fees of repairing and maintaining the landscaped and communal areas of the estate.

The Court held that incidental benefit was not sufficient for the enforcement of a burden against one who had not himself covenanted for it and that the benefit of a positive covenant would only be enforced against the successor in title of the covenantor if (but not to the extent that) he chose to exercise the corresponding right.

Broomleigh Housing Association Ltd v Hughes (1999)

A tenant in a block of flats covenanted to contribute proportionately to the service charge and the landlord covenanted to keep the property in good repair.

The landlord replaced windows in other flats, but not those in the tenant's flat as these had been recently replaced at the tenant's own expense.

Notwithstanding that the replacement of the windows in the tenant's flat did not constitute a breach of covenant as the landlord has subsequently given the requisite consent, it was held that this did not reduce or vary the obligation upon the tenant to contribute to the total service charge. There was no provision in the lease to allow for this to happen.

Furthermore, the fact that the landlord might have waived the obligation to contribute for some tenants, that is to say those who had obtained a prior written consent, does not create any right or expectation that other tenants should be treated in the same way provided the waiver did not increase the liability of other tenants and any loss arising from such a waiver falls upon the landlord.

Billson and others v Tristrem (2000)

A tenant of a basement flat of a property divided into five flats covenanted to pay 20 per cent of the proportion of the costs of maintaining entrances, passages, landings and staircases 'enjoyed or used by the lessee in common'. The tenant was held to be liable for payment of a proportion of the costs of maintaining the main entrance even though access to the basement flat was by way of separate entrance and the tenant did not have a right to use the main entrance. In this case, whilst the wording of the lease was considered to be inappropriate, the tenants' proportions of the service charge was specified as 20 per cent per flat and therefore the tenant was liable to contribute towards the landlord's total costs relating to the building even though the costs included items from which the tenant received no direct benefit.

Pattrick and another v Marley Estates Management Ltd (2007)

A tenant held a 999-year lease of premises that originally formed part of a manor house estate divided into 17 separate dwellings. The demised premises consisted of four floors on the west side of the original manor house, together with the terraces of cloisters and nine acres of parkland. The cloisters were left when the adjoining abbey was demolished as part of the redevelopment of the house.

The tenant was liable to pay 14 per cent of the running costs of the mansion house.

The Court held that the cloisters fell within the definition of the building and were therefore within the landlord's repairing obligations even though the cloisters were only used (and useable) by the lessees. The Court made the observation that the same could be said of other parts of the 'building' where the cost of upkeep and repair would fall within the service charge but would not always benefit each lessee equally.

1.6.2 A tenant could be liable for the cost of performing the same service twice

Even if a tenant performs a service for itself, it might still be liable for a proportion of the cost of the same or similar service performed by the landlord.

St Modwen Developments (Edmonton) Ltd v Tesco Stores Ltd (2007)

St Modwen acquired the freehold reversion to premises in the Edmonton Green shopping centre from the borough council. The landlord brought proceedings to establish its entitlement to: (i) service charges certified by its finance director in place of the borough treasurer; (ii) a contribution to the cost of refuse collection for other tenants, in circumstances where the tenant disposed of its own refuse; and (iii) a 10 per cent management fee.

On the issue of waste removal from the common parts, the landlord was acting within the provisions of the lease that related to keeping the common parts clean, notwithstanding that the presence of the waste might arise from a breach by a different tenant under another contract. Moreover, the removal of waste for the purpose of the overall management, cleanliness and control of the buildings came legitimately within the scope of the proviso.

1.7 SWEEPER CLAUSES

When drafting a lease for, say, a term of 20 years, the landlord may not be able to predict with certainty what services will be supplied in the future. As technology advances and tenant expectations change, it might be appropriate for additional services to be provided during the term of the lease. For instance, CCTV may be installed to augment and improve security but the technology may not have existed when the lease was originally granted. Hence, the ability for the landlord to recover the costs of providing, maintaining and repairing a CCTV installation could not have been included within the original service charge provisions.

To avoid the risk of the landlord incurring future costs that might fall outside of the service charge, many service charges contain a 'sweeper clause'.

1.7.1 A sweeper clause is intended to cover future services not envisaged by the parties when granting the lease

A properly drafted sweeper clause would entitle the landlord to charge for additional services not foreseen or in contemplation when the lease was granted and which might be provided in the future for the benefit of the building and its proper maintenance and servicing.

Sun Alliance and London Assurance Co Ltd v British Railways Board (1989)

Leases granted in respect of a building provided that the tenants were responsible for external window cleaning. The landlord had actually carried out this service as it was not possible for the tenant to carry out the cleaning in compliance with the *Health and Safety at Work Act* 1974. The tenant had accepted the position and had reimbursed the landlord the costs incurred in cleaning the exterior of the windows over a number of years. The landlord replaced a 'ramshackle' arrangement for gaining access to the windows with a modern automated system requiring additional works to strengthen the roof.

The tenant covenanted to contribute towards:

> 'The cost of providing such other services as the lessor shall consider ought properly and reasonably to be provided for the benefit of the building, or for the proper maintenance and servicing of any part or parts thereof.'

It was held that the landlord had 'properly and reasonably' considered that the improved window-cleaning service was one that ought to be provided for the benefit of the building and its proper maintenance and servicing. Notwithstanding the fairly heavy capital cost involved in the new installation, the landlord was entitled to recover the contributions demanded from the tenants.

The landlord's position was, however, helped as they had not sought recovery of the total cost of the new window-cleaning cradle. The new system was clearly an upgrading or improvement from the existing one. To the extent that the new system was a replacement of the old, the cost was recoverable although the proportion of the landlord's costs attributable to the upgrading of the system was not claimed.

Ashley Gardens Freeholds Ltd v Cole (2007)

The external redecorations of wooden window frames in a block of flats included the application of a proprietary pre-paint system which was held to be works of repair and not therefore recoverable under the relevant service charge provision as a decoration cost. However, the landlord was entitled to recover the costs as work being 'necessary or advisable for the proper maintenance safety and administration of the Building'.

1.7.2 A sweeper clause cannot make good a drafting defect

A sweeper clause cannot be used to make good a drafting defect in the lease nor can it be used to create an additional obligation on the part of the tenant to pay for a service that was in contemplation at the date of the grant of the lease but was not included within the service charge provisions.

If the lease allows additions or variations to the services at the landlord's reasonable discretion, it will not generally enable the landlord to increase the scope of the main provisions of the service charge clause.

Mullaney v Maybourne Grange (Croydon) Management Co Ltd (1986)

A landlord replaced defective old wooden-framed windows in a tenant's flat with new double-glazed windows. The landlords undertook to repair and maintain and otherwise provide services and amenities to the structure and common parts of the block. The tenant covenanted to contribute to the costs of so doing and to such further or additional costs as the defendants incurred in 'providing and maintaining additional services or amenities'. The landlord claimed that installation of the new windows was a repair or that, alternatively, the expenditure was incurred in 'providing and maintaining additional services or amenities'. It was held that the replacement of the old windows was not a repair but a long-term improvement and although the new windows had attributes that made them desirable, they could not be regarded in the ordinary sense as an 'amenity'.

Jacob Isbicki & Co Ltd v Goulding & Bird Ltd (1989)

The tenant covenanted to pay a service charge being a proportion of the expenses incurred by the landlord in the repair, maintenance and insurance of the building and the provision of services set out under a separate schedule of the lease. The list of heads of expenditure set out in the schedule did not include sandblasting to the external walls. There was a proviso giving the landlord discretionary powers to add to or make any alteration in the rendering of the services so listed.

The landlord claimed the tenant was liable to contribute to the expenditure on the external walls on the basis that the landlord could vary the service charge. It was held that the power given to the landlord to vary the services was a limited one within the range of the works mentioned in the schedule, not a right to impose liability on the tenant in respect of different kinds of works.

Lloyds Bank plc v Bowker Orford (1992)

The tenant covenanted to pay a service charge being the due proportion of the total cost to the lessor of providing, amongst other things, a lift service, a caretaker, security, cleaning and lighting of common parts, cleaning and lighting of lavatories, constant hot water, and 'any other beneficial services which may properly be provided by the lessee'.

There was a specific landlord's covenant to repair the outside of the building but no reference to repairs in the list of services for which the landlord was entitled to recover.

The landlord sought to recover the costs of external repairs and internal decoration and repairs of the common parts of the building.

It was held that a proportion of the cost of external repairs and internal decorations and repairs of the common parts were not recoverable as not being 'beneficial services'.

The landlord was under an obligation to carry out external repairs and if it had intended to recover the costs it would have been very simple to reserve the right by reference to it in the list of service charges.

Therefore, if the landlord has in mind the provision of a service, but he has not covered the right to include the cost of providing it in the service charge, he will not generally be able to argue that he has the power to provide the service under the sweeper clause and to recover the cost.

Fluor Daniel Properties Ltd v Shortlands Investment Ltd (2001)

Leases of a modern commercial block required the landlord to maintain equipment and to provide air-conditioning and other services. The air-conditioning system was well maintained and in good working order. The landlord sought to recover £2m under the service charge provisions for upgrading the system. The landlord sought to rely on the wording of the repairing covenant which gave the landlord express power to make reasonable additions and variations to the services.

It was held that the cost of the works was not recoverable as the service charge provisions of the lease presupposed some defect or disrepair to the equipment had to exist prior to the need for replacement. As no defect existed which required that the system be replaced, and the proposed works were not required to maintain the service, the costs were not recoverable.

Mason v TotalFinaElf (2003)

The tenant covenanted that it would 'to the satisfaction of the Lessor's Surveyor well and substantially uphold support maintain amend repair decorate and keep in good condition the demised premises'.

The landlord brought a claim for dilapidations and it was held that reference to the works being 'to the satisfaction of the Landlord's Surveyor' entitled the landlord's surveyor to prescribe what works should be done and the manner in which the work was to be performed. However, it did not give the landlord's surveyor carte blanche to determine what was required; the works had to be to make good a want of repair or absence of good condition.

Whilst a dilapidations case, the decision in this instance may also be relevant to sweeper provisions in terms of the performance of works or services which are at the discretion of the landlord.

1.7.3 Clarifying the intent and meaning of a sweeper clause

Where the scope of the sweeper clause is unclear, the landlord is advised to seek agreement with the tenants, failing which he should apply to the courts for a declaration.

Reston Ltd v Hudson (1990)

Timber window frames were found to be defective and it was more satisfactory and cheaper to replace all the timber windows at the same time than to leave it to individual tenants to do so from time to time. An issue arose as to the responsibility for replacement and whether the cost would be covered by the service charge.

The lessor covenanted to repair the windows and structures of the estate other than those for which the lessees were responsible. The service charge payable included 'cost and expenses incurred by the lessor' including the matters for which the lessor was responsible under the repairing covenants.

The lessor sought to first circularise the tenants to inform them of the proposals and, having received certain objections from some tenants, took the precaution of going to the Court for an appropriate declaration.

It was held that the replacing of the windows would be properly recoverable under the service charge.

1.7.4 Recovering the cost of arrears recovery

In the absence of express wording, a sweeper clause entitling the landlord to recover the costs of other services which the lessor may at its discretion provide, is unlikely to extend to the inclusion of legal fees incurred in connection with the recovery of arrears.

St Mary's Mansions Ltd v Limegate Investment Co Ltd (2002)

A lease entitled the landlord to recover the costs of 'all other services which the lessor may at its absolute discretion provide' and the reasonable and proper fees for general management of the property. It was held that the wording of the lease did not entitle the landlord to recover legal costs of proceedings to recover arrears.

1.8 LIABILITY AFTER LEASE EXPIRY

Tenants will generally only be liable for costs expended during the term of the lease.

Capital & Counties Freehold Equity Trust Ltd v BL plc (1987)

A tenant of an office building covenanted to pay a proportion of costs and expenses in respect of repair and decoration of common parts and the exterior 'which may from time to time during the said term be expended or incurred or become payable'. The landlord contracted with builders to carry out repairs and redecorations to the exterior and common parts before the end of the term. However, no part of the works had in fact been carried out by the end of the term. It was held that only services that were provided during the term were chargeable.

1.9 CONSULTATION WITH TENANTS

Landlord and Tenant Act 1985

For residential dwellings, s. 20(4) of LTA 1985 requires prior consultation with tenants and also provides that tenants must be given written warnings in respect of any costs which will be included in a demand which will be served on them more than 18 months after the costs are incurred.

The LVT has discretion to dispense with the consultation requirements if it is satisfied that the landlord has acted reasonably or if emergency works are required where following the requirement to serve notice would be detrimental to the interests of the tenants.

Commonhold and Leasehold Reform Act 2002

Section 151 of CLRA 2002 modifies the existing s. 20 of LTA 1985 and gives leaseholders rights to be consulted before landlords enter into long-term agreements (where one contractor is appointed to carry out works, provide a service, etc. for a period of more than one year) and where the cost per dwelling is more than £100 *and* before entering into a 'long-term agreement' of over 12 months costing more than £250 per dwelling.

The requirements came into force on 31 October 2003 and are set out in the *Service Charges (Consultation Requirements) (England) Regulations* 2003 (SI 2003/1987).

Failure to consult with tenants in accordance with the regulations *will* result in the landlord being unable to recover more than the prescribed amount.

1.9.1 Where a lease includes both residential and commercial premises, the statutory regulations designed to protect residential occupiers will still need to be followed

Where the lease contains both residential and commercial premises the commercial service charge would in effect no longer be governed solely by the law of contract but could also benefit from the statutory regulation usually only afforded to residential tenants.

Heron Maple House Ltd v Central Estates Ltd (2002)

This case involved the freehold of a building incorporating retail, office, residential and commercial premises. Central Estates held a head-lease of the residential element of the building which included various common areas, plant rooms, etc. Central Estates in turn had granted an under-lease to Camden Council of the same premises. In turn, Camden granted various tenancies to individual occupier tenants.

The freeholder carried out substantial works to the building and sought recovery through the service charge. However, neither the freeholder nor the intermediate landlord followed the consultation procedures set down under s. 20 and it was subsequently argued that s. 20 only applied to service charges payable by a tenant of a dwelling; which did not include Central Estates or Camden whose premises included other areas of the building.

The judge held that there was nothing in the Act that requires a tenant of a dwelling to be in actual occupation and that in relation to any individual flat/dwelling both Central Estates and Camden were the tenant of that dwelling. The s. 20 procedures were therefore needed to be followed all the way down the chain of tenants.

Oakfern Properties Ltd v Ruddy (2006)

This case involved a building consisting of commercial premises on the lower floors and separate residential flats on the upper floors. The upper floors were let by the freeholder on a long-lease and the flats were separately sub-let.

A sub-tenant sought to challenge the amount of the maintenance charge levied by the freeholder on the ground that the amount was unreasonable within the meaning of LTA 1985.

It was held that the purpose of s. 18–430 of LTA 1985 was to protect a residential tenant against excessive or unreasonable service charges.

A 'tenant of a dwelling' within the meaning of s. 38 of LTA 1985 was not excluded from the protection afforded to residential tenants merely because, whilst he was the tenant of a dwelling which extended only to part of a building, he was also the tenant of other parts of the building. LTA 1985 speaks of the 'tenant of a dwelling' not the 'tenant of a dwelling and nothing else'.

1.9.2 Section 20 notices must have regard to the total costs of works

If works are to be carrying out as a single project but comprise separate distinct items, a s. 20 notice will be required to be served if the total cost of the works exceeds the prescribed limit.

Martin v Maryland Estates Ltd (1999)

The lessees of a Victorian house, converted into residential flats, covenanted to reimburse the landlord the cost of repair and other maintenance works.

The landlord carried out external repairs and followed the consultation process under s. 20 of LTA 1985. However, additional works were also carried out. The new works related partly to works which were indirectly covered by the earlier s. 20 notice; partly to works which were the tenants direct responsibility; and partly to works to which s. 20 was relevant but where no notice had been served.

The landlord sought recovery on the basis that the additional works could be viewed as separate items each being below the limit for which a s. 20 notice would be needed and that, furthermore, s. 20(9) of the Act applied in that notice was not required as compliance with s. 20 would have caused delay resulting in an increase in the cost of the works.

It was held that the tenants were not liable for the full sums claimed in view of the lack of service of further s. 20 notices. Furthermore, no power under s. 20(9) arose as the landlord had made a conscious decision not to inform the tenants of the additional expenditure and in doing so had acted unreasonably.

1.9.3 Requirement to serve s. 20 notices in respect of emergency repairs

The requirement to serve prior notice may be set aside by the LVT if, acting reasonably, the landlord has not served notice and the works are required to be carried out as a result of an emergency where the tenant would suffer hardship if works were to be delayed.

Wilson v Stone (1998)

Structural damage was discovered requiring urgent remedial works to prevent a potential danger of collapse of the building and contractors already on site were instructed to proceed with the necessary work.

The tenant was liable for a proportion of the costs as it was held that the landlord had acted reasonably in accepting the advice given and in instructing a reputable builder already on site; the charge was reasonably incurred and the cost not excessive.

1.9.4 Serving of notice as a condition precedent

Where a lease sets down clear and unambiguous conditions, for consultation with tenants prior to incurring expenditure, the landlord would be unable to recover the expenditure even though the tenants were aware of the landlord's intention to incur costs.

CIN Properties Ltd v Barclays Bank plc (1986)

An agreement obliged the tenant to pay a proportion of the costs of repairs subject to the proviso that the landlord would not accept any estimates or place orders for work without first submitting them to the tenant for approval. The landlord placed orders for the carrying out of extensive works without consulting the tenant. The Court of Appeal held that the proviso was an unequivocal condition precedent to the tenant's liability.

Northways Flats Management Co (Camden) v Wimpey Pension Trustees (1992)

The tenant of ground floor commercial premises covenanted to pay a service charge in respect of works of repair. The lease provided that in respect of major works, the landlord was to submit a copy of the specification of works and estimates obtained to the tenant for consideration and, in the event the tenant did not raise objections within 21 days, the tenant shall be deemed to have accepted the specification and estimates as reasonable. It was held that the costs of works carried out were not recoverable as there was a specific obligation upon the landlord that was an essential part of the mechanism for the resolution of disputes.

2
Recoverable costs

2.1 REIMBURSEMENT OF COSTS ONLY

The word 'costs' is not a precise legal term. It can be limited to payments actually made, expenses incurred but not yet paid; and can even mean income foregone.

Agavil Investment Co v Corner (1975)

Under Clause 3 of the lease a landlord covenanted, amongst other things, to employ a caretaker for the building whether resident upon the demised premises or otherwise.

The tenant covenanted to reimburse the landlord ⅛ of costs and expenses incurred in connection with the maintenance, replacement, renewal and insurance of the lift and ⅟₁₈ of costs, expenses and outgoings, and matters mentioned in the schedule.

The schedule included:

'(1) the costs, charges and expenses incurred by the lessor in carrying out its obligations under cl. 3;

(2) all rates, taxes, charges, assessments, impositions and outgoings payable in respect of the caretaker's accommodation; and

(3) the expenses of management and of the services provided by the lessor for the general benefit of the tenants … and all other expenses reasonably incurred by the lessor in or in connection with or relating to the buildings the communal gardens caretaker's accommodation the garages refuse bins the demised premises of the garden store.'

It was held that a notional rent for the caretaker's flat was recoverable within the meaning of 'costs or expenses' incurred. Alternatively, the cost fell clearly within (3) – 'all other expenses reasonably incurred'.

Cleve House Properties Ltd v Schidlof (1980)

It was held that the landlords were not entitled to claim a management fee where the landlords' directors in fact performed the management functions gratuitously, so that no actual expenditure was incurred.

Russel v Laimond Properties Ltd (1984)

Under the lease, the landlord could recover the cost of providing porterage services including the cost of providing, maintaining and repairing a porter's flat. The landlord sought a declaration to include the annual rental value of the resident porter's flat. The judge held that cost means cost, that is to say, money laid out and does not mean lost revenue or income, which is foregone. But, cost (in the sense of money laid out) might include either interest paid or a reasonable return on the capital employed in providing the flat. However, the declaration required by the landlord was not given as insufficient information was available to enable a determination of what that 'cost' might be.

Lloyds Bank plc v Bowker Orford (1992)

The tenant covenanted to pay a service charge being the due proportion of the total cost to the lessor of providing, amongst other things, a lift service, a caretaker, security, cleaning and lighting of common parts, cleaning and lighting of lavatories, constant hot water, and 'any other beneficial services which may properly be provided by the lessee'.

The landlord sought to recover the notional cost of providing accommodation in the building for a caretaker.

It was held that the landlord was entitled to claim a notional rent in respect of accommodation in the building for a caretaker on the basis that the notional rent was a cost in the sense of money foregone as opposed to money spent.

2.2 RECOVERABILITY OF COSTS NOT YET PAID

A landlord may commit to expenditure and the works may be completed but an invoice not paid at the end of the service charge period. In such circumstances, costs may not have been expended and there is some debate as to whether, at this point, costs have been 'incurred'.

Dependent upon the strict wording of the lease, the landlord would generally be able to recover the costs of works and services completed or supplied but not yet paid.

There is, however, a distinction between monies which have not yet been paid and those which are not yet due.

Capital & Counties Freehold Equity Trust Ltd v BL plc (1987)

A tenant of an office building covenanted to pay a proportion of costs and expenses in respect of repair and decoration of common parts and the exterior 'which may from time to time during the said term be expended or incurred or become payable'. The landlord contracted with builders to carry out repairs and redecorations to the exterior and common parts before the end of the term. However, no part of the works had in fact been carried out by the end of the term. It was held that only services that were provided during the term were chargeable.

Gilje and others v Charlegrove Securities Ltd (2000)

Leases of flats contained a covenant for the landlord to provide a resident housekeeper. Whilst the obligation to provide a resident housekeeper included an obligation to provide the residence, the landlord was not entitled to recover a notional rent of the caretaker's flat, as the notional rent was not 'monies expended' within the operative part of the service charge provisions.

Barrington v Sloane Properties Ltd (2007)

The landlord of a block of flats contracted to carry out substantial building works over a three-year period. The lease provided for the tenant to pay 24.24 per cent of the 'actual cost' to the landlord of providing the services and for such sum to be certified annually by the landlord's accountant, such certificate to be conclusive.

The works contract was supervised by an architect who valued the work from time to time and issued certificates for payment. Each certificate was subject to a 5 per cent retention and the balance was payable within 14 days of the certificate.

The landlord's accountant certified the service charge for each year based on the estimated value of the works carried out rather than the amount which had actually been charged and become payable in each service charge year.

The Lands Tribunal held that 'actual cost' was limited to sums that had fallen for payment in each year and did not include the cost of works undertaken but not yet payable.

2.3   NOTIONAL COSTS

Many leases contain provision for the landlord to include a notional or deemed rent in respect of accommodation provided for use by staff employed on site. However, unless the lease specifically provides for a notional rent to be included within the service charge, caution is needed if seeking to include a notional rent within the service charge.

Service charge costs are normally limited to actual costs expended, although income foregone could amount to a 'cost' or 'expense' but is not regarded as 'monies expended'. Therefore the detailed wording of the service charge clause would need to be carefully examined.

Agavil Investment Co v Corner (1975)

Under Clause 3 of the lease a landlord covenanted, amongst other things, to employ a caretaker for the building whether resident upon the demised premises or otherwise.

The tenant covenanted to reimburse the landlord ⅛ of costs and expenses incurred in connection with the maintenance, replacement, renewal and insurance of the lift and 1/18 of costs, expenses and outgoings, and matters mentioned in the schedule.

The schedule included:

'(1) the costs, charges and expenses incurred by the lessor in carrying out its obligations under cl. 3;

(2) all rates, taxes, charges, assessments, impositions and outgoings payable in respect of the caretaker's accommodation; and

(3) the expenses of management and of the services provided by the lessor for the general benefit of the tenants ... and all other expenses reasonably incurred by the lessor in, or in connection with, or relating to, the buildings the communal gardens caretaker's accommodation the garages refuse bins the demised premises of the garden store.'

It was held that a notional rent for the caretaker's flat was recoverable within the meaning of 'costs or expenses' incurred. Alternatively, the cost fell clearly within (3) – 'all other expenses reasonably incurred'.

Russel v Laimond Properties Ltd (1984)

Under the lease, the landlord could recover the cost of providing porterage services including the cost of providing, maintaining and repairing a porter's flat. The landlord sought a declaration to include the annual rental value of the resident porter's flat. The judge held that cost means cost, that it to say, money laid out and does not mean lost revenue or income, which is foregone. But, cost (in the sense of money laid out) might include either interest paid or a reasonable return on the capital employed in providing the flat. However, the declaration required by the landlord was not given as insufficient information was available to enable a determination of what that 'cost' might be.

Lloyds Bank plc v Bowker Orford (1992)

The tenant covenanted to pay a service charge being the due proportion of the total cost to the lessor of providing, amongst other things, a lift service, a caretaker, security, cleaning and lighting of common parts, cleaning and lighting of lavatories, constant hot water, and 'any other beneficial services which may properly be provided by the lessee'.

The landlord sought to recover the notional cost of providing accommodation in the building for a caretaker.

It was held that the landlord was entitled to claim a notional rent in respect of accommodation in the building for a caretaker on the basis that the notional rent was a cost in the sense of money foregone as opposed to money spent.

Gilje and others v Charlegrove Securities Ltd (2000)

Leases of flats contained a covenant for the landlord to provide a resident housekeeper. Even though the obligation to provide a resident housekeeper included an obligation to provide the residence, the landlord was not entitled to recover a notional rent of the caretaker's flat, as the notional rent was not 'monies expended' within the operative part of the service charge provisions.

3
Services

3.1 GENERAL

3.1.1 Services, amenities and conveniences

Where the provision in the lease uses such words as 'services', 'amenities' or 'conveniences', the interpretation of that word will depend upon the context.

Mullaney v Maybourne Grange (Croydon) Management Co Ltd (1986)

A landlord replaced defective old wooden-framed windows in a tenant's flat with new double-glazed windows. The landlord undertook to repair and maintain and otherwise provide services and amenities to the structure and common parts of the block. The tenant covenanted to contribute to the costs of so doing and to such further or additional costs as the defendants incurred in 'providing and maintaining additional services or amenities'. The landlord claimed installation of the new windows was a repair or alternatively that the expenditure was incurred in 'providing and maintaining additional services or amenities' to the block. It was held that the replacement of the old windows was not a repair but a long-term improvement and although the new windows had attributes that made them desirable, they could not be regarded in the ordinary sense as an 'amenity'.

Jacob Isbicki & Co Ltd v Goulding & Bird Ltd (1989)

The tenant covenanted to pay a service charge being a proportion of the expenses incurred by the landlord in the repair, maintenance and insurance of the building and the provision of services set out under a separate schedule of the lease. The list of heads of expenditure set out in the schedule did not include sand-blasting to the external walls. There was a proviso giving the landlord discretionary power to add to or make any alteration in the rendering of the services so listed.

The landlord claimed the tenant was liable to contribute to the expenditure on the external walls on the basis that the landlord could vary the service charge to include works of repair to the external walls. It was held that the power given to the landlord to vary the services was a limited one within the range of the works mentioned in the schedule, not a right to impose liability on the tenant in respect of different kinds of works.

Lloyds Bank plc v Bowker Orford (1992)

The tenant covenanted to pay a service charge being the due proportion of the total cost to the lessor of providing, amongst other things, a lift service, a caretaker, security, cleaning and lighting of common parts, cleaning and lighting of lavatories, constant hot water, and 'any other beneficial services which may properly be provided by the lessee'.

The landlord sought to recover the costs of employing managing agents to carry out and provide the specified services and the notional cost of providing accommodation in the building for a caretaker.

It was held that the landlord was entitled to recover the cost of employing managing agents to organise and supervise the provision of services and to claim a notional rent in respect of accommodation in the building for a caretaker.

Daejan Properties Ltd v Bloom (2000)

The tenant of a basement garage, located beneath a courtyard serving a block of 109 flats, covenanted to pay a reasonable proportion of the charges for rebuilding, repairing and cleansing all walls, fences, drains and other 'conveniences' belonging to the premises and capable of being used by the lessee in common with the owners or occupiers of adjoining or contiguous premises.

It was held that the tenant was responsible for the cost of works to replace the asphalt membrane to the concrete slab, which comprised the roof of the garage premises and on which the forecourt and the flats were built, as this was a 'convenience' within the meaning of the lease.

3.1.2 Landlord's discretion as to how services are performed

Where a landlord covenants to perform certain services or works it is usually for the landlord, acting reasonably, to decide the method of complying with his covenant.

Manor House Drive Ltd v Shahbazian (1965)

A landlord covenanted to 'maintain, repair and decorate the main structure and roof of the building'. A leak occurred in the roof and the landlord's surveyor recommended replacement of the roof covering. The tenants claimed that a cheaper, less permanent repair could have been carried out. It was held that the works undertaken were a reasonable and proper way of maintaining the roof. Even though a permanent repair would not make a great financial saving, even in the long term, the landlord was entitled to undertake repairs that were reasonable and proper.

Stent v Monmouth District Council (1987)

A dwelling house which stood in an exposed location suffered constant ingress of water blown through or under the front door. The landlord carried out various remedial works over time without success, including replacement of the whole door. The problem was eventually resolved when the door was replaced with an aluminium self-sealing door unit. The tenant was awarded damages for the landlord's breach of covenant to maintain and repair the structure and exterior.

The landlord appealed on the grounds that the water penetration did not result from disrepair but to an inherent defect. It was held that: (i) the fact the door did not fulfil its function was ipso facto a defect for the purpose of the repairing covenant; (ii) the door had itself become damaged, had rotted and become out of repair; and (iii) the replacement of the wooden door with the self-sealing aluminium door was a sensible and practical repair which should have been carried out much earlier.

Mason v TotalFinaElf (2003)

The tenant covenanted that it would 'to the satisfaction of the Lessor's Surveyor well and substantially uphold support maintain amend repair decorate and keep in good condition the demised premises '.

The landlord brought a claim for dilapidations and it was held that reference to the works being 'to the satisfaction of the Landlord's Surveyor' entitled the landlord's surveyor to prescribe what works should be done and the manner in which the work was to be performed. However, it did not give the landlord's surveyor carte blanche to determine what was required and, if acting reasonably, the surveyor came to a decision that a reasonable surveyor could reach, it would not matter if the tenant would prefer a cheaper, but no less reasonable, option.

3.2 PROVISION OF ON-SITE STAFF

A landlord may expressly covenant to provide porterage or caretaking staff or the provision of such services may be at the landlord's discretion.

If the landlord wishes to recover costs of staffing, the lease should make specific reference. However, reference to salaries and wages may not include other incidental expenses such as National Insurance contributions, pension contributions, etc.

Hupfield v Bourne (1974)

The landlord of a block of luxury flats covenanted to:

> '... employ such persons as shall be reasonably necessary for the due performance of the landlord's covenants and for the proper management of the block.'

The landlord had, for a period of 11 years, employed a resident caretaker occupying a flat on the lower ground floor. The landlord sought to sell the flat and sacked the resident caretaker, substituting a firm of contractors to carry out the caretaker's cleaning duties and disposal of rubbish. The tenant brought an action seeking a declaration that, under the terms of the lease, the landlord was bound to provide the services of a resident porter and also sought an injunction restraining the landlord from selling the porter's flat. It was held that in the context of a luxury block of flats, the services of a residential caretaker were 'reasonably necessary' for the performance of the landlord's covenants and proper management of the block.

Russel v Laimond Properties (1984)

Under the lease, the landlord was entitled to recover the cost of providing porterage services including the cost of providing, maintaining and repairing a porter's flat. It was held that the fact that the landlord could recover such costs did not impose an obligation upon the landlord to provide a resident porter.

Posner v Scott-Lewis (1987)

A landlord of a block of flats covenanted:

> 'To employ (so far as in the Lessor's power lies) a resident porter for the following purposes and for no other purpose:
>
> (a) to keep clean the common staircases and entrance hall landings and passages and lift;
>
> (b) to be responsible for looking after and stoking the central heating and domestic hot water boilers; and
>
> (c) to carry down rubbish from the properties to the dustbins outside the building every day.'

A porter, resident in the building for many years, ceased to be employed by the lessor and vacated the flat. However, he continued to carry out his former duties on a part-time basis whilst resident elsewhere. It was held that whilst the duties of the porter continued to be performed, the landlord was in breach of covenant in failing to provide a resident porter. The tenant benefited from the feeling of security; a resident porter was valued not only for his actual duties but for his very presence and an order for specific performance was granted.

3.3   STAFF ACCOMMODATION

3.3.1   Notional rent

Often contentious, the costs of providing accommodation for staff can go beyond simple maintenance, repair and other outgoings (e.g. rates/council tax, electricity and gas, etc.) but sometimes also extends to notional rent.

Agavil Investment Co v Corner (1975)

Under Clause 3 of the lease a landlord covenanted, amongst other things, to employ a caretaker for the building whether resident upon the demised premises or otherwise.

The tenant covenanted to reimburse the landlord ⅛ of costs and expenses incurred in connection with the maintenance, replacement, renewal and insurance of the lift and ¹⁄₁₈ of costs, expenses and outgoings, and matters mentioned in the schedule.

The schedule included:

'(1) the costs, charges and expenses incurred by the lessor in carrying out its obligations under cl. 3;

(2) all rates, taxes, charges, assessments, impositions and outgoings, payable in respect of the caretaker's accommodation; and

(3) the expenses of management and of the services provided by the lessor for the general benefit of the tenants … and all other expenses reasonably incurred by the lessor in, or in connection with, or relating to, the buildings the communal gardens caretaker's accommodation the garages refuse bins the demised premises of the garden store.'

It was held that a notional rent for the caretaker's flat was recoverable within the meaning of 'costs or expenses' incurred. Alternatively, the cost fell clearly within (3) – 'all other expenses reasonably incurred'.

Lloyds Bank plc v Bowker Orford (1992)

The tenant covenanted to pay a service charge being the due proportion of the total cost to the lessor of providing, amongst other things, a lift service, a caretaker, security, cleaning and lighting of common parts, cleaning and lighting of lavatories, constant hot water, and 'any other beneficial services which may properly be provided by the lessee'.

The landlord sought to recover the notional cost of providing accommodation in the building for a caretaker. It was held that the landlord was entitled to claim a notional rent in respect of accommodation in the building for a caretaker.

3.3.2 Notional rent is not 'money expended'

Gilje and others v Charlegrove Securities Ltd (2000)

Leases of flats contained a covenant for the landlord to provide a resident housekeeper. Even though the obligation to provide a resident housekeeper included an obligation to provide the residence, the landlord was not entitled to recover a notional rent of the caretaker's flat, as the notional rent was not 'monies expended' within the operative part of the service charge provisions.

3.3.3 No implied obligation to provide staff

A covenant enabling a landlord to recover the cost of staff accommodation does not, in the absence of specific wording, impose an obligation on a landlord to provide a resident porter/caretaker.

Russel v Laimond Properties Ltd (1984)

Under the lease, the landlord could recover the cost of providing porterage services including the cost of providing, maintaining and repairing a porter's flat. It was held that the fact that the landlord could recover such costs did not impose an obligation upon the landlord to provide a resident porter.

3.4 INSURANCE

It is now more common for the recovery of costs incurred by the landlord in insuring the building against fire and other perils to be a wholly and distinctly separate recoverable item, outside of the usual 'service charge' provisions for recovery of the cost of other services, repairs and maintenance, etc.

Because insurance premiums can be large one-off payments, not spread throughout the service charge period, landlords usually now prefer tenants to reimburse the costs of insuring the building 'on demand'.

However, plant and machinery and other miscellaneous insurances such as public liability insurance, etc. may still be recovered with costs of other services, repairs and maintenance, etc.

Commonhold and Leasehold Reform Act 2002

Section 151 of CLRA 2002 modifies the existing s. 20 of LTA 1985 and gives leaseholders rights to be consulted before landlords enter into long-term agreements (where one contractor is appointed to carry out works, provide a service, etc. for a period of more than one year) and where the cost per dwelling is more than £100 and before entering into a contract to carry out works costing more than £250 per dwelling.

Insurance could well fall under the s. 151 provisions and require prior consultation with tenants.

The requirements came into force on 31 October 2003 and are set out in the *Service Charges (Consultation Requirements) (England) Regulations* 2003 (SI 2003/1987).

Failure to consult with tenants in accordance with the regulations *will* result in the landlord being unable to recover more than the prescribed amount.

3.4.1 Landlord not obliged to accept lowest quote

In respect of commercial property, where a lease qualifies the landlord's covenant to insure, the landlord is not obliged to seek alternative quotations or to accept the cheapest quotation.

Bandar Property Holdings v JS Darwen (Successors) Ltd (1968)

A landlord covenanted to insure premises against specified risks 'in some insurance office of repute'. The tenants obtained a lesser quote for identical insurance to that effected by the landlord. The Court held that a term obliging the landlord to place the insurance so as not to impose an unnecessarily heavy burden on the tenants could not be implied.

Havenridge Ltd v Boston Dyers (1994)

A lease obliged tenants to pay sums that the landlord shall 'properly expend or pay to any insurance company in respect of ... insuring ... the demised premises'. The Court held that 'properly' meant legitimately and that it was neither necessary nor clearly intended that there should be an implication of reasonableness. Provided the insurance was effected in accordance with the terms of the lease (i.e. placed with an insurer 'of repute'), the contract was negotiated at arm's length and the rate was representative of the market value, the landlord was not obliged to seek alternative cheaper quotes.

Berrycroft Management Co Ltd v Sinclair Gardens Investments (Kensington) Ltd (1997)

Leases of a block of flats imposed a requirement on the management company to insure the building for such sums and through such companies as the landlord may direct. The lessees covenanted to pay an appropriate proportion of the insurance cost. It was held that there was no implied covenant that the sum charged by the insurers should be reasonable or that a tenant should not be required to pay a substantially higher sum than he could himself arrange. It was also found that the amounts charged were neither unreasonable nor excessive and were in line with market rates.

For residential premises and the purposes of s. 19(2A) of LTA 1985, the question is not whether the expenditure is the cheapest available, but whether the charge made was reasonably incurred.

Forcelux Ltd v Sweetman (2001)

The landlord incurred expenditure on insurance, maintenance and management fees which it sought to recover as service charge items. The tenants referred the charges to the LVT under s. 19(2A) of LTA 1985. On appeal the Lands Tribunal held that s. 19(2A) was not concerned with whether costs were 'reasonable' but whether they were 'reasonably incurred'.

On the question of insurance, whilst the tenants were penalised because cover for commercial landlords was more expensive than that available to owner-occupiers, it was for the landlord to insure and this was not an option for the tenants. The landlord's block policy had been competitively obtained in accordance with market rates and accordingly the costs of insurance premiums were reasonably incurred.

3.4.2 Landlord obliged to reinstate in the absence of funds

Where a landlord covenants to insure, he may be required to make good any damage caused even though he has not yet received any insurance monies from the insurers.

Vural Ltd v Security Archives Ltd (1990)

The tenant of factory premises agreed to pay, as additional rent 'the fair and proper proportion' of the premiums paid by the landlord in keeping the premises insured. The landlord covenanted to insure against loss or damage by fire and such other 'risks and perils as the landlord might deem expedient'. The wooden floor of the premises sustained fire damage and the landlord deliberately delayed reinstating the floor in the hope of persuading the tenant to give up the lease. The landlord subsequently proposed to lay a heavy-duty industrial linoleum floor but the tenant refused to grant access, as he wanted the original wooden floor reinstated. The tenant eventually renewed the wooden floor and sued for damages for breach of covenant.

It was held that the landlord was obliged to exercise the rights conferred by a policy of insurance financed by the tenant in such a way as to preserve the tenant's interests in what he had paid for. An obligation to pursue a claim was therefore to be implied. With regard to the replacement of the flooring it was also held that, whilst a slavish reconstruction of what was originally there was not an inevitable ingredient in reinstatement, if the original material was appreciably more effective, a substitute would, in general, not constitute reinstatement, even though better value for money.

3.4.3 Liability for shortfall resulting from excess or exclusion

If one party to the lease provides an unqualified covenant to insure for the full reinstatement costs of the premises, he may be liable for any shortfall in the full reinstatement value resulting from any excess or exclusion or if cover against certain risks is not available.

Enlayde Ltd v Roberts (1917)

The tenant covenanted to repay sums expended by the landlord pursuant to a covenant to insure the demised premises against loss or damage by fire and to keep the property in repair 'except in the case of destruction or damage by fire'. In the event of damage by fire, the landlord covenanted to lay out all monies received in respect of such insurance in rebuilding or reinstating the premises and in the event such monies should be insufficient would 'make good such insufficiency out of her own moneys'. Incendiary bombs dropped by enemy aircraft destroyed the premises. The insurance policy effected excluded loss or damage resulting from 'invasion, foreign enemy ... military or usurped power'. Although policies usually exempted damage caused by military action, it was held that the words 'loss or damage by fire' must be construed in a strict sense and the landlord was held to be liable for the loss that had occurred.

Upjohn v Hitchens (1918)

A tenant covenanted to insure the demised premises against loss or damage by fire 'in the Imperial Insurance Company or in some other responsible office in London or Westminster to be previously approved by the lessor'. Through the agency of the lessor, the premises were insured under a policy that excepted loss or damage by 'invasion, foreign enemy ... military or usurped power'. As a consequence of enemy raids, the landlord required the tenant to insure also against loss or damage by fire occasioned by enemy action in pursuance of the tenant's covenant. The tenant refused and the landlord commenced proceedings to recover possession.

It was established that the named company and other insurance offices in London and Westminster had never insured against aircraft risks and their policies had always excluded such risks. It was held that the covenant was to effect such a policy as was the usual policy of the companies in question at the date of the lease and therefore there had been no breach of covenant by the tenant.

Moorgate Estates Ltd v Trower (1940)

Mortgagors covenanted to keep premises insured against loss of damage by missiles or projectiles from or fired at aircraft. It was also provided that, should they fail to do so, the mortgagees might insure at the expense of the mortgagors and furthermore that the mortgagees power of sale should immediately become exercisable in the event of a breach of any of the mortgagors' covenants.

Unbeknown to both parties, the insurance policy effected did not comply with the covenant although at the time such a policy was obtainable. Such policies were, however, subsequently made unavailable. On becoming aware of the defect in the insurance, the mortgagees served notice to pay off the mortgage. It was held that there had been a breach of covenant since there was no implied term in the contract that if it became impossible to obtain a policy of insurance in accordance with the contract neither party should be entitled to rely on failure to comply with the contract.

3.4.4 If a landlord insures to obtain cheaper cover, this will not vary tenant covenant to insure

Where a landlord is able to procure more cost effective insurance and subsequently insures, notwithstanding a tenant's positive covenant to do so, in the absence of formal documentation of the arrangement, the tenant will continue to remain liable.

Argy Trading Developments v Lapid Developments (1977)

Under the terms of an under-lease for six years, a tenant of warehouse premises covenanted to keep the premises insured against loss or damage by fire and to reinstate the premises. However, the landlord insured the building under a block policy covering other properties and the tenant paid the landlord the appropriate proportion of the premium.

The landlord did not subsequently renew the policy and the insurance lapsed. Shortly after, the premises were damaged by fire requiring the demolition of part of the building.

The premises were scheduled for redevelopment and neither the freeholder nor the tenant's direct landlord wished for the premises to be reinstated. The tenant, however, had four years left on the under-lease and wanted to continue using the premises.

It was held that there had been no contract between the parties as to the insurance and accordingly it was impossible that any terms could be implied to the effect that the landlord would maintain the block policy or would not cancel the policy without giving notice to the tenant. The duty of care was merely a duty not to negligently give advice.

3.5 VARIATION OF SERVICES

Part IV of LTA 1987 allows variation in certain circumstances upon application to the courts if the lease fails to make satisfactory provision: (i) for repair and maintenance of a flat or building; (ii) for repair and maintenance of installations or services; (iii) for the recovery of expenditure incurred; or iv) for the computation of the service charge.

With effect from 30 September 2003, CLRA 2002 has passed jurisdiction for such matters from the county court to the LVT.

For commercial properties, the wording of the lease allowing the landlord to vary the provision of services is predominant.

3.5.1 Variation of non-discretionary services

A landlord's ability to vary or discontinue a service will be limited only so far as the lease allows. A landlord may be held to be in breach of covenant in failing to provide a service, which could result in an award of damages or an order of specific performance to restore the provision of the service.

Posner v Scott-Lewis (1987)

A landlord of a block of flats covenanted:

'To employ (so far as in the Lessor's power lies) a resident porter for the following purposes and for no other purpose:

(a)   to keep clean the common staircases and entrance hall landings and passages and lift;

(b)   to be responsible for looking after and stoking the central heating and domestic hot water boilers; and

(c)   to carry down rubbish from the properties to the dustbins outside the building every day.'

All flat leases contained a similar provision to the effect that the lessor would recover all expenditure incurred under this covenant.

A porter, resident in the building for many years, ceased to be employed by the lessor and vacated the flat. However, he continued to carry out his former duties on a part-time basis whilst resident elsewhere. It was held that whilst the duties of the porter continued to be performed, the landlord was in breach of covenant in failing to provide a resident porter. The tenant benefited from the feeling of security; a resident porter was valued not only for his actual duties but for his very presence and an order for specific performance was granted.

3.5.2 Variation of discretionary services

If a service is provided voluntarily and not pursuant to a specific covenant or obligation, it could be withdrawn, apparently without notice.

Argy Trading Developments v Lapid Developments (1977)

Under the terms of an under-lease for six years, a tenant of warehouse premises covenanted to keep the premises insured against loss or damage by fire and to reinstate the premises. However, the landlord insured the building under a block policy covering other properties and the tenant paid the landlord the appropriate proportion of the premium.

The landlord did not subsequently renew the policy and the insurance lapsed. Shortly after, the premises were damaged by fire requiring the demolition of part of the building.

The premises were scheduled for redevelopment and neither the freeholder nor the tenant's direct landlord wished for the premises to be reinstated. The tenant, however, had four years left on the under-lease and wanted to continue using the premises.

It was held that there had been no contract between the parties as to the insurance and accordingly it was impossible that any terms could be implied to the effect that the landlord would maintain the block policy or would not cancel the policy without giving notice to the tenant. The duty of care was merely a duty not to negligently give advice.

3.5.3 Variation of services at lease renewal

Where a business lease is renewed under the *Landlord and Tenant Act* 1954, the landlord may be able to update the lease to seek limited recovery or, when an existing service charge regime exists, to amend the service charge provisions into a more modern standard form.

However, a landlord could not impose a full service charge recovery lease where previously the lease did not make provision.

O'May v City of London Real Property Company Ltd (1982)

A landlord sought inclusion of a more onerous (for the tenant) service charge provision on renewal of a lease following contractual expiry. The landlord was prepared to reduce the rent to reflect the transfer of risk and the burden of services and repairs from the landlord to the tenant.

The tenant was successful in obtaining a new lease substantially upon the same terms as the old lease. The decision of the Court of Appeal was affirmed in the House of Lords that the landlord had to demonstrate the change was fair and reasonable having regard to the comparatively weak negotiating position of the sitting tenant. It was not sufficient to show that the reduction in rent was adequate compensation but that it was fair and reasonable for the change to be made and for the fluctuating burden of unpredictable service charges to be imposed on the tenants against their will.

3.5.4 Variation resulting from change in statute

If the method or manner of the provision of a service is varied by statute, resulting in the landlord incurring increased or additional costs, such costs may not be recoverable unless the service charge provisions specifically allow for it.

This is of topical relevance as a landlord who may be required to carry out improvement works in order to comply, for example, with the *Disability Discrimination Act* 1995. The landlord may not be able to recover the costs through the service charge if the lease does not contain a provision relating to the costs of complying with statute and/or the cost of making improvements.

Frobisher (Second Investments) Ltd v Kiloran Trust Co Ltd (1980)

A lease provided for payment in advance of interim sums on account of service charges that were paid into a separate bank account maintained by the landlord's managing agents.

It was held that the interim sums were a service charge to which s. 91A(1)(b) of the *Housing Finance Act* 1972 applied. This provides that a service charge is only recoverable from a tenant once the landlord had defrayed the cost, or at least incurred liability for the cost, of the chargeable item. It followed, therefore, that the landlord was not entitled to require the interim payments to be made in advance on account of estimated or proposed expenditure.

Deprived of the ability to collect payment in advance, the landlord sought to recover the cost of borrowing money to meet its obligations under the lease.

It was held that the fees payable to the landlord's managing agents were paid for carrying out the general management and administration of the property which, on the true construction of the leases, could not include interest paid on money borrowed. Nor could a term be implied in the lease as a matter of necessary implication that, in the event of supervening legislation rendering the payment of the service charge in advance unlawful, the tenant was to pay interest. The doctrine of implying a term to give efficacy to an agreement did not apply where there had been a disturbance to the contractual arrangement resulting from statute. Then it must be left to the statute to say what is to happen consequentially on its intervention, and that one cannot foist on the parties what some outside body thinks would have been what they would have agreed to in circumstances that neither of them could possibly have contemplated under any circumstances.

Broadwater Court Management Company Ltd v Jackson-Mann (1997)

Service charge provisions in respect of leases of a block of flats did not expressly include costs relating to annual auditing and filing of statutory returns under the *Companies Act* 1989. A company established by the tenants to acquire the freehold of the block sought to recover such costs within the service charge but were prevented from doing so as the leases made no specific provision and the recovery of such costs were not intended at the time the leases were granted.

3.6 LANDLORD'S FAILURE TO PROVIDE SERVICES

In the case of residential leases, a landlord has certain obligations that are implied by statute.

Landlord and Tenant Act 1985

In the case of tenancies of under seven years, s. 13 of LTA 1985 imposes an obligation for the landlord to be responsible, at his own cost, for keeping in repair: (i) the exterior and structure of the dwelling; (ii) the water, gas, electrical and sanitation installations in the dwelling; and (iii) the installations in the dwelling for space heating and hot water.

In the case of residential tenancies to which s. 13 does not apply and commercial property, leases will usually set out the covenants and obligations of both landlord and tenants.

However, it is becoming increasingly common in commercial leases, for a service charge clause to contain a list of services and works the cost of which the landlord can recover but which the landlord can provide entirely at his discretion. The landlord may not, therefore, be bound by a direct covenant to actually provide the services or works.

Where a landlord fails to provide services or carry out works, careful reading of the lease is required to establish whether the landlord is under a positive covenant to provide them and whether a failure to carry out works or provide certain services constitutes a breach of covenant.

3.6.1 Landlord's obligation irrespective of funding

The landlord may be in breach of covenant to provide services irrespective of funding and whether tenants have actually paid any interim service charges demanded. Damages for breach of covenant, based upon the diminution in the value of each demise, could therefore be many times the actual cost of remedying the breach.

Marenco v Jacramel (1964)

A landlord covenanted to keep and maintain the exterior of a block of 12 flats in good repair and condition and properly maintained including the entrances, passageways, staircases, fences, etc.

The tenant covenanted to pay a proportion of the costs of insuring the building and a fair proportion of the cost of keeping clean and lighting the entrance and staircase and to contribute a rateable or due proportion of the expense of making, repairing, maintaining, etc. the exterior of the building, fences, etc.

The tenant served notice on the landlords requiring them to carry out various works for which they were responsible. The landlords were not, however, prepared to carry out the works until the other lessees of the block had contributed to the cost of previous works and given security for future contributions.

It was held that the landlords were in breach of covenant and that the fact that other tenants had not paid their service charges did not alter the landlords' obligation to comply with their covenants.

It was also held that the amount of damages was to be based on the cost for the whole block and the original trial judge was wrong to divide the cost of the works by the number of flats. The landlords were therefore potentially liable to each tenant for the same sum, i.e. 12 times the total cost of the works.

Electricity Supply Nominees v National Magazine Co (1999)

A landlord of a seven-storey office block covenanted to use its reasonable endeavours to provide and carry out as economically as may be reasonably practicable various services including lift services and air-conditioning. The tenant sought damages in respect of an excessive rate of breakdowns and occasions of defective operation of the lifts and air-conditioning. The measure of damages for breach of the covenant to provide the services was held to be the resultant diminution in value to the tenant of its occupation of the premises.

However, if a tenant wilfully withholds payment which itself causes the landlord's inability to perform its obligations, the position will be different and the tenant denied equitable relief.

Bluestorm Ltd v Portvale Holdings Ltd (2004)

A subsidiary company of Portvale was the freeholder of a block of flats who also acquired the leasehold interest in 35 out of a total of 57 flats in the block. The building was in a poor state of repair. Two tenants successfully obtained judgment against the landlord for damages for breaches of the landlord's repairing covenants. The landlord company was then dissolved and the freehold was acquired by Bluestorm, a company controlled by the tenants of the 22 flats unconnected with Portvale.

Portvale then gave notice to Bluestorm alleging breach of the landlord's repairing covenants and withheld payment of the rent and service charge. Portvale counterclaimed for damages for the dilapidated state of the building.

The county court gave judgment to Bluestorm which was upheld at the Court of Appeal. The decision, on the face of it, appears to be contrary to the decision in *Yorkbrook Investments v Batten* (1985), however, the court found that the tenant's refusal to pay resulted in the landlord's inability to perform and whilst the claim might be equitable in its origins and nature, Portvale should be denied equitable relief as the dilapidated state of the building was originally due to Portvale's subsidiary company's neglect of the building prior to the acquisition by Bluestorm.

3.6.2 Effective date of breach

There is a general rule that a covenant to keep in repair requires that the premises should not fall into disrepair. A covenantor will therefore be in breach of the obligation immediately a defect occurs. There is an exception, however, where the obligation is the landlord's and the defect occurs in the demised premises themselves. In such circumstances, the landlord is only in breach when he has information about the existence of the defect and then subsequently fails to carry out the necessary works with reasonable expedition.

However, where the defect occurs in premises not comprised in the demised premises, the landlord is considered to be in breach as soon as the defect occurs.

British Telecom plc v Sun Life Assurance Society plc (1996)

A landlord covenanted to keep the building as a whole 'in complete good and substantial repair and condition'. A bulge appeared in the brick cladding. When the landlord was informed of the disrepair he immediately erected scaffolding and temporary protection. Remedial works commenced some 17 months later.

It was held that the landlord was in breach of covenant as soon as the property became in disrepair, and not at the later time when he had information about the existence of the defect and had failed to carry out the necessary repairs with reasonable expedition, since the exception to the general rule only applied where the defect occurred in the demised premises themselves and not where it occurred in part of the premises not demised to the tenant.

Wallace v Manchester City Council (1998)

Manchester City Council were obliged, under s. 11 of the LTA 1985, to keep in repair the structure and exterior of a dwelling. The premises suffered disrepair consisting of a collapsed wall, rotten windows, a failed damp-proof course, loose plaster and skirtings, rat infestation and leaking rainwater pipes. The tenant alleged that disrepair had been evident since 1992. In December 1996, the Council carried out repairs to replace a window and re-point a wall but were unable to gain access to carry out further works.

However, the first documentary reference to a complaint was made in October 1994. It was held that that the proper period of breach, for which damages were to be awarded, was for the period commencing from October 1994.

3.6.3   Mitigation of damages for landlord's breach of covenant

Where a landlord is possibly in breach of covenant, the savings in not carrying out earlier remedial works may, in appropriate circumstances, mitigate the amount of damages.

Postel Properties Ltd v Boots the Chemist Ltd (1996)

Landlords carried out repairs to low-level roofs and upper windows of a large shopping centre. The tenants argued that the work to the windows was due to rust, which could have been contained with timeous maintenance and redecoration.

It was held that the works to the windows and cladding were repairs, and, in so far as the landlord may have been guilty of delay in carrying out such works, that was more than balanced by the saved costs of earlier repainting.

3.6.4 Consequential losses resulting from landlord's breach

If a landlord fails to comply with an obligation to repair, as a result of which additional repairs and damage is caused, the landlord will not be able to recover the additional costs under the service charge.

Loria v Hammer (1989)

A landlord sub-divided a building into four flats and was responsible for repairs to the flat roof of an extension on which water tanks were located. As a result of the landlord's failure to repair the tank housing, water penetrated through cracks and splits in the asphalt under the tanks causing wet and dry rot and damage to the decorations to the flat below.

The landlord failed to carry out repairs despite having received notice of the defects from the tenants. The tenants then proposed carrying out the remedial works and claimed damages. The landlord agreed to the tenants carrying out the works so long as this was at their own expense.

It was held that the tenant's action of carrying out works to remedy the defects did not amount to waiver or estoppel preventing the tenants from reclaiming the money from the landlord and that the landlord was not able to increase the service charge by reason of its own default in delaying repair and thus adding to the expenditure required.

Daejan Properties Ltd v Bloom (2000)

The tenant of a basement garage, located beneath a courtyard serving a block of 109 flats, covenanted to pay a reasonable proportion of the charges for rebuilding, repairing and cleansing all walls, fences, drains and other 'conveniences' belonging to the premises and capable of being used by the lessee in common with the owners or occupiers of adjoining or contiguous premises.

It was held that if it were to be established that works carried out by the lessor over the years had damaged the asphalt membrane, that the proportion of the damage should not be the responsibility of anyone other than the landlord.

3.6.5 Latent defects

In the event of a latent defect, giving rise to disrepair, a landlord may not be liable for a failure to repair if he had not previously been aware of the defect.

O'Brien v Robinson (1973)

By virtue of s. 32(1)(a) of the *Housing Act* 1961, the landlord of a dwelling house was under an implied covenant to keep the structure of the dwelling in repair. A ceiling collapsed as a result of a latent defect causing injury to the tenant. Neither the landlord nor the tenant was previously aware of the existence of the latent defect. It was held that the landlord, whilst responsible for repairing the ceiling, was not liable for damages caused as a result of the ceiling falling in. Under the statutory implied covenant, the landlord's obligation to carry out repairs did not arise until he had information of the existence of the defect and had had a reasonable opportunity to carry out remedial works. As the disrepair resulted from a latent defect, the tenant was not in a position to bring the defect to the landlord's attention and therefore the landlord could not be held to be in breach of covenant.

3.6.6 Change of circumstances

Due to a change in circumstances, a landlord may be required to adapt services, even though the need for change was outside of the landlord's control, to ensure that tenants are not deprived of the service completely.

O'Connor v Old Etonian Housing Association Ltd (2002)

As part of a refurbishment, the landlord replaced water pipework with pipes of a smaller bore. Some years later, the local water pressure fell due to an increased local demand and the pipes were found to be inadequate to supply water to the top floor of the premises.

The problem would not have arisen if the pipes had been replaced with a similar diameter to the original or if a pump had been installed. The problem was not rectified for some years when the Water Authority restored pressure following the construction of a new pumping station.

The landlord covenanted to 'keep in proper working order'. The Court held that it would be wholly unreasonable for a landlord to leave his tenants deprived of a satisfactory supply for a lengthy period simply for want of modest expenditure on modifications.

3.6.7 Variation of services

A landlord's ability to vary or discontinue a service will be limited only so far as the lease allows. A landlord may be held to be in breach of covenant in failing to provide a service, which could result in an award of damages or an order of specific performance to restore the provision of the service.

Posner v Scott-Lewis (1987)

A landlord of a block of flats covenanted:

'To employ (so far as in the Lessor's power lies) a resident porter for the following purposes and for no other purpose:

(a) to keep clean the common staircases and entrance hall landings and passages and lift;

(b) to be responsible for looking after and stoking the central heating and domestic hot water boilers; and

(c) to carry down rubbish from the properties to the dustbins outside the building every day.'

All flat leases contained a similar provision to the effect that the lessor would recover all expenditure incurred under this covenant.

A porter, resident in the building for many years, ceased to be employed by the lessor and vacated the flat. However, he continued to carry out his former duties on a part-time basis whilst resident elsewhere. It was held that whilst the duties of the porter continued to be performed, the landlord was in breach of covenant in failing to provide a resident porter. The tenant benefited from the feeling of security; a resident porter was valued not only for his actual duties but for his very presence and an order for specific performance was granted.

4
Repairs, renewals, replacements and improvements

The precise wording of the lease may have a considerable impact upon the obligations of the respective parties to the lease. The distinction between repair and improvement is often very fine and it is not uncommon for less scrupulous landlords to seek to carry out refurbishment or improvement works under the pretext of repair and maintenance.

The law relating to repair is extensive and the wording of the definitions within the lease is crucially important; particularly in relation to repair and the definition of the demise and retained parts.

It is essential, therefore, to clearly define the extent of the demise and the extent of what remains the landlord's responsibility.

Landlord and Tenant Act 1985

Sections 8–17 of LTA 1985 impose obligations on landlords and limits or prohibits the recovery of costs from tenants in respect of certain types of letting, e.g. lettings of houses at low rents, short tenancies for under seven years, etc.

In respect of houses let on low rents to which s. 8–10 apply, the landlord is under an implied obligation, at his own cost, to put and keep the house in a condition fit for human habitation.

In respect of tenancies granted for less than seven years (s. 11–13), landlords are liable, at their own cost, to keep in repair the structure and exterior of the building including drains, and to keep in repair and in proper working order the installations for the supply of utilities and the installations in the dwelling for the provision of heating and hot water.

4.1 REPAIRS

'Repair' has been defined as the rectifying of damage or deterioration in putting back into good condition something that, having been in good condition, has fallen into bad condition.

Repair is the restoration by renewal or replacement of subsidiary parts of a whole. Renewal, as distinguished from repair, is reconstruction of the entirety, meaning not necessarily the whole but substantially the whole subject matter under discussion.

4.1.1 Disrepair must be present

In order for the cost of repairs to be recoverable, there must first be an element of disrepair.

Quick v Taff-Ely Borough Council (1986)

A house built in the early 1970s suffered severe condensation caused by a lack of insulation around the concrete window lintels, sweating from the single-glazed metal-frame windows and inadequate heating. The tenant brought an action, requiring the landlord to replace the windows and face the concrete lintel, under the statutory covenant to repair implied by s. 32(1) of the *Housing Act* 1961 that required the local authority to keep in repair the structure and exterior.

It was held that disrepair related to the condition of whatever had to be repaired and not a lack of amenity and that there had to be disrepair before any question arose to whether it would be reasonable to remedy a design fault. Since there was no evidence of damage or want of repair, the landlord was not in breach of the implied repairing covenant.

Post Office v Aquarius Properties Ltd (1987)

The tenant covenanted to keep premises in good and substantial repair. As a result of an original construction defect, when the water table rose, the basement became flooded. The water table subsequently fell leaving the basement once again dry and apart from letting in water, no other damage was caused to the building. The defect had not grown worse but was in the same condition as it was when the building was first built.

The Court held that the tenant's obligation only arose when the property was in a state of disrepair. As the defect had existed since construction of the building and there had been no worsening or deterioration of the condition of the premises, no want of repair existed and therefore no liability arose on the part of the tenant.

Fluor Daniel Properties Ltd and others v Shortlands Investments Ltd (2001)

Leases of a modern commercial block required the landlord to maintain equipment and to provide air-conditioning and other services. The air-conditioning system was well maintained and in good working order. The landlord sought to recover £2m under the service charge provisions for upgrading the system. The landlord sought to rely on the wording of the repairing covenant, which gave the landlord express power to make reasonable additions and variations to the services.

It was held that the cost of the works was not recoverable as the service charge provisions of the lease presupposed some defect or disrepair to the equipment had to exist prior to the need for replacement. As no defect existed which required that the system be replaced, and the proposed works were not required to maintain the service, the costs were not recoverable.

Mason v TotalFinaElf (2003)

This was a dilapidations case where the tenant covenanted that it would 'to the satisfaction of the Lessor's Surveyor well and substantially uphold support maintain amend repair decorate and keep in good condition the demised premises'. The landlord brought a claim for dilapidations and it was held that:

(1) The wording of the covenant presupposed that the item in question suffered from some defect, physical damage, deterioration or malfunctioning such that repair amendment or renewal was necessary.

(2) There was no authority for the proposition that purely anticipatory, preventative work, where no damage or deterioration in the condition had yet occurred, could be called for or the reasonable cost of it recovered. The fact that a piece of equipment was old, and would inevitably have to be replaced in time, did not mean preventative works could be required to prevent the consequence of the equipment failing where, in the meantime, it continued to perform its function.

4.1.2   Maintaining in good condition and repair

A covenant to maintain in 'good condition' may result in a liability even though a state of disrepair does not exist.

Welsh v Greenwich London Borough Council (2000)

A tenancy agreement in respect of a flat in a purpose-built block obliged the landlords 'to maintain the dwelling in good condition and repair'. The flat suffered excessive condensation caused by inadequate insulation resulting in severe black spot mould growth. It was held that reference to 'good condition' conveyed a separate concept to the word 'repair'. Whilst there was no damage or disrepair to the structure, the mould was caused by a lack of adequate insulation and therefore the landlord had failed to maintain the flat in good condition.

4.1.3   Fair wear and tear

The landlord may not be able to recover the cost of repairs that go beyond fair wear and tear where the cause of the repair resulted from the landlord's actions (or inaction).

Daejan Properties Ltd v Bloom (2000)

The tenant of a basement garage, located beneath a courtyard serving a block of 109 flats, covenanted to pay a reasonable proportion of the charges for rebuilding, repairing and cleansing all walls, fences, drains and other 'conveniences' belonging to the premises and capable of being used by the lessee in common with the owners or occupiers of adjoining or contiguous premises.

It was held that if it were to be established that works carried out by the lessor over the years had damaged the asphalt membrane, that the proportion of the damage should not be the responsibility of anyone other than the landlord. Conversely, in so far as any part of the damage to the membrane had been caused by incorrect laying in the first instance, or wear and tear over the years, this would fall under the repairing covenant for which the lessee was responsible.

Continental Property Ventures Inc v White (2006)

Leases in respect of a block of flats contained provision for recovery of service charges in respect of expenditure by the landlord on, inter alia, repairs.

The issue before the Lands Tribunal was an appeal against an earlier LVT decision as to whether a number of items of service charge expenditure had been 'reasonably incurred' within the meaning of s. 19(1)(a) of LTA 1985.

It was held: (i) that the cost of damp-proofing works on the ground floor were disallowed as they should have been carried out at no charge under a guarantee; and (ii) only £3,525 of repairs to one of the flats, carried out at a cost of £17,114 had been reasonably incurred as a result of the landlords neglect in repairing a leaking pipe.

4.1.4 Repair means repair

If the service charge provisions refer only to repair, then works beyond the scope of repair will fall outside the charge. Unless expressly referred to, the landlord will generally be unable to recover the cost of improvements under the definition of repair.

Mullaney v Maybourne Grange (Croydon) Management Co Ltd (1986)

A landlord replaced defective old wooden-framed windows in a tenant's flat with new double-glazed windows. The landlords undertook to repair and maintain and otherwise provide services and amenities to the structure and common parts of the block.

The tenant covenanted to contribute to the costs of so doing and to such further or additional costs as the defendants incurred in 'providing and maintaining additional services or amenities'.

The landlord claimed installation of the new windows was a repair or alternatively that the expenditure was incurred in 'providing and maintaining additional services or amenities' to the block. It was held that the replacement of the old windows was not a repair but a long-term improvement and although the new windows had attributes that made them desirable, they could not be regarded in the ordinary sense as an 'amenity'.

Sutton (Hastoe) Housing Association v Williams (1988)

The tenant of a block of flats covenanted to pay a service charge being a proportion of the costs of various matters including within the lessor's covenants as follows:

'5(1)(a)(i) maintaining, repairing, renewing and in all ways keeping in good condition the Block ...

5(1)(a)(viii) carrying out such works and providing such additional works and services as may be considered necessary by the lessor in its absolute discretion from time to time.'

The lease made reference to a Schedule of Condition and a Schedule of Repairs to the structure anticipated during the next ten years that stated:

'External timber elements will need to be renewed during the next ten years. This includes windows, timber cladding to fascias and garage doors.'

Wet rot in the woodwork of windows had caused leaks and had required constant repairs. The housing association decided to replace the old single-glazed wooden windows with double-glazed uPVC windows.

The tenant appealed an earlier county court judgment that did not distinguish between repairs and improvements. The county court judge's finding was upheld that there was no need to as the replacement of the windows, whether amounting to repair or including an element of improvement, was covered by the wording under section 5(1)(a) of the lease, whether under subsection (i) or (viii).

Although not disagreeing with the decision in *Mullaney v Maybourne Grange* above, because of the terms of the lease the question of whether the work could be both repair and improvement did not arise.

4.1.5 Recovery of costs of improvements that reduce cost of repair

In the absence of specific wording, the cost of improvements may be recoverable if the works carried out are intended to have a long-term effect of reducing the cost of repairs.

Postel Properties Ltd v Boots the Chemist Ltd (1996)

Landlords carried out repairs to low-level roofs and upper windows of a large shopping centre. The flat low-level roofs, which were constructed in 1975 and 1976 with a maximum life expectancy of 20 years, were re-covered under a phased programme. The tenants argued that the replacement of the roof covering was premature and the specification was increased to a point where there was an irrecoverable excess, and that the work to the windows was due to rust which could have been contained with timeous maintenance.

It was held that the repairs to the roof were repairs that a reasonably minded building owner might undertake and they did not amount to giving back to the landlord something different from that which existed before. It was reasonable to commence them when the landlord did, notwithstanding that some parts had not yet failed. The works to the windows and cladding were repairs, and, in so far as the landlord may have been guilty of delay in carrying out such works, that was more than balanced by the saved costs of earlier repainting.

Wandsworth London Borough Council v Griffin (2000)

A block of flats were constructed with flat roofs and had metal-framed windows which were in disrepair. Wandsworth London Borough Council replaced the flat roofs with pitched roofs and the windows with uPVC double-glazed units. It was held that within the meaning of the Council's repairing obligations, the works constituted repair as they were cheaper than the alternatives, taking into account both initial and future costs and that the decision to replace the flat roofs with pitched roofs and the windows with uPVC double-glazed units was a reasonable one.

4.1.6   Overlapping obligations

Where a landlord and tenant have repairing obligations, a court will try to interpret the lease so as to avoid overlapping repairing obligations, making only one party responsible for the relevant item of repair.

Jacey v de Sousa (2003)

The Court refused to impose an obligation on the landlord to carry out repairs to drains, even though the lease entitled him to recover these costs as part of the service charge.

Pattrick v Marley Estates Management (2007)

A tenant held a 999-year lease of premises that originally formed part of a manor house estate divided into 17 separate dwellings. The demised premises consisted of four floors on the west side of the original manor house, together with the terraces of cloisters and nine acres of parkland. The cloisters were left when the adjoining abbey was demolished as part of the redevelopment of the house.

The tenant was liable to pay 14 per cent of the running costs of the mansion house.

Substantial repairs were required to the majority of the windows and to the cloisters. The two main issues related to whether the landlord or tenant was responsible for repairs to the cloisters and for the repair and redecoration of some 25 Georgian style windows to the premises.

The tenant claimed the windows were part of the main structure of the building and therefore the liability for repair fell to all the tenants collectively as part of the service charge. The lease made clear that the windows were part of the premises.

It was held that the windows were not included in the definition of the structure of the building and therefore the tenant was responsible for repair and renewal of the windows. However, the lease placed responsibility for redecoration of the exterior of the houses and buildings on the landlord and therefore the landlord was liable for external redecoration of the windows.

The Court also held that the cloisters did fall within the definition of the building and were therefore within the landlord's repairing obligations even though the cloisters were only used (and useable) by the lessees. The Court made the observation that the same could be said of other parts of the 'building' where the cost of upkeep and repair would fall within the service charge but would not always benefit each lessee equally.

4.2 FIXTURES AND FITTINGS

A 'fixture' means something that is affixed to the premises after the structure is completed. It does not include things that form part of the original structure itself.

Boswell v Crucible Steel Co of America (1925)

A tenant occupied business premises, the sides of which mainly consisted of non-opening plate-glass windows, covenanted 'to keep the inside of the demised premises including all landlord's fixtures in good repair'. The landlord covenanted to 'repair ... the demised premises with all necessary reparations ... except such repairs as are hereby agreed to be executed by the lessees'.

A number of windows were vandalised and the landlord served notice upon the tenant to instigate repairs on the basis that the windows were landlord's fixtures. It was held that, in the particular circumstances, the windows formed part of the structure and could not therefore be considered to be landlord's fixtures but part of the walls.

4.3   EXTENT OF REPAIR WORKS

4.3.1   The landlord has discretion as to the works required to comply with his repairing obligation

Whether the landlord is required to carry out temporary or more major permanent repairs will depend upon the defect and what is reasonable in the circumstances. Where a landlord covenants to perform certain services or works it is usually for the landlord, acting reasonably, to decide the method of complying with his covenant.

Manor House Drive Ltd v Shahbazian (1965)

A landlord covenanted to 'maintain, repair and decorate the main structure and roof of the building'. A leak occurred in the roof and the landlord's surveyor recommended replacement of the roof covering. The tenants claimed that a cheaper, less permanent repair could have been carried out. It was held that the works undertaken were a reasonable and proper way of maintaining the roof. Even though a permanent repair would not make a great financial saving, even in the long term, the landlord was entitled to undertake repairs that were reasonable and proper.

Stent v Monmouth District Council (1987)

A dwelling house which stood in an exposed location suffered constant ingress of water blown through or under the front door. The landlord carried out various remedial works over time without success, including replacement of the whole door. The problem was eventually resolved when the door was replaced with an aluminium self-sealing door unit. The tenant was awarded damages for the landlord's breach of covenant to maintain and repair the structure and exterior.

The landlord appealed on the grounds that the water penetration did not result from disrepair but to an inherent defect. It was held that: (i) the fact the door did not fulfil its function was ipso facto a defect for the purpose of the repairing covenant; (ii) the door had itself become damaged, had rotted and become out of repair; and (iii) the replacement of the wooden door with the self-sealing aluminium door was a sensible and practical repair which should have been carried out much earlier.

Murray v Birmingham City Council (1987)

There was an implied covenant under s. 32 of the *Housing Act* 1961 (now replaced by s. 11–16 of LTA 1985) for the landlord to carry out repairs to the roof. The landlord had carried out periodic repairs over time. It was held that the roof was capable of being repaired by periodic attention and had not yet reached the stage when the only practical remedial action was replacement of the roof as a whole.

4.3.2 Amending, rebuilding and renewing

Additional wording such as 'amend', 'rebuild' and 'renew' may widen the scope of works beyond a strict interpretation of 'repair' and may include remedying inherent defects. A covenant to keep premises 'in good and tenantable condition' may also extend an obligation beyond normal repairs.

Credit Suisse v Beegas Nominees Ltd (1994)

The landlord of a building erected in 1977 covenanted by cl. 5(c) (subject to payment of a service charge representing 75 per cent of the costs) 'to maintain repair amend renew... and otherwise keep in good and tenantable condition ... the structure ... roof ... and walls'. The tenant's premises experienced leaks through the cladding panels due to a design defect.

The water leaks had become worse owing to the movement of the panels and failure of the seals at the joints.

It was held that the landlord was in breach of cl. 5(c). The requirement to keep the premises in 'good and tenantable repair' meant that the building would be substantially watertight. Therefore, replacement of the cladding was within cl. 5(c) as it was not substantial rebuilding and although it went beyond 'repair', it fell within the obligation to 'renew and amend'.

Welsh v Greenwich London Borough Council (2000)

A tenancy agreement in respect of a flat in a purpose-built block obliged the landlords 'to maintain the dwelling in good condition and repair'. The flat suffered excessive condensation caused by inadequate insulation resulting in severe black spot mould growth. It was held that reference to 'good condition' conveyed a separate concept to the word 'repair'. Whilst there was no damage or disrepair to the structure, the mould was caused by a lack of adequate insulation and therefore the landlord had failed to maintain the flat in good condition.

4.3.3 The length of the lease may determine what is reasonable

If works are established as constituting 'repair' rather than 'improvement' the landlord may need to consider the extent of the works in the context of the length of the leases.

Scottish Mutual Assurance plc v Jardine Public Relations Ltd (1999)

The tenant occupied part of the second floor of an office block under a three-year lease. The landlord carried out only short-term repairs to the roof, intended to deal with immediate leakage problems. The landlord then carried out more extensive repair work and sought recovery of a proportion of the costs from the tenant.

The Court ruled that the tenant was only liable to pay a proportion of the service charge demanded. Whilst accepted as repairs and not improvements, the landlord was only entitled to recover the costs of complying with its repairing obligation over the period of the lease, not the cost of works carried out in performance of the landlord's obligations over a longer term. The fact that the lease was close to expiry was a contributing factor but this does not give tenants the authority that, as a general rule, they cannot be required to pay higher service charge for works carried out towards the end of the term. If a landlord can demonstrate that repairs are necessary to comply with its obligations under the terms of the lease, and within the life of the lease, the costs are likely to be recoverable even from a tenant whose lease is about to end.

Fluor Daniel Properties Ltd and others v Shortlands Investments Ltd (2001)

Leases of a modern commercial block required the landlord to maintain equipment and to provide air-conditioning and other services. The air-conditioning system was well maintained and in good working order. The landlord sought to recover £2m under the service charge provisions for upgrading the system. The landlord sought to rely on the wording of the repairing covenant which gave the landlord express power to make reasonable additions and variations to the services.

On the question of reasonableness, it was held that the standard had to be such as the tenants, given the lengths of their lease, could fairly be expected to pay for and the landlord could not reasonably overlook the relatively limited interest of the paying tenants. If the landlord wished to carry out repairs which go beyond those which the tenants, given their more limited interest, can be fairly expected to pay, then, subject always to the terms of the lease, the landlord must bear the additional costs himself.

4.4 STRUCTURAL AND EXTERNAL REPAIRS

There is no statutory or legal definition of what constitutes the 'structure' or 'exterior'. The definition will often be different from case to case dependent upon the physical attributes of the building. However, in respect of tenancies to which s. 11–13 of LTA 1985 apply, the 'structure and exterior' means all those parts of the building belonging to the landlord and not just the structure and exterior of the demised premises.

4.4.1 Additional works consequential to structural works

A covenant to repair the structure may extend to an obligation to carry out further necessary works consequential to the structural works.

Smedley v Chumley & Hawkes Ltd (1982)

The landlord of a timber-framed building, located near a riverbank, covenanted:

> 'To keep the main walls and roof in good structural repair and condition throughout the term and to promptly make good all defects due to faulty materials or workmanship in the construction of the premises.'

The tenant covenanted:

> ' . . . well and substantially to repair, maintain and keep the interior and exterior of the premises in good order and condition.'

The building was built on a concrete raft supported by piles at the river end, but not at the other. The unsupported end of the raft had sunk causing the raft to tilt.

The landlord carried out the remedial work to the foundations by driving in additional piles to support the raft. When the work was done, the premises were the same in the sense that the superstructure was the same as it had been when first built, although the foundations were different.

The tenant brought an action seeking an order that the landlord should carry out works to repair the cracking to the main walls and defects to the roof that had resulted from the earlier subsidence. The landlord pleaded that any defects in the premises were a direct consequence of the design and so outside the scope of the repairing covenant.

The landlord was held to be responsible for the further remedial works required to the walls and roof. When construing a covenant to repair, the state in which the building was in at the date of the lease and the precise terms of the lease should be looked at in order to decide if work could be termed 'repair'. The landlord's obligation to keep the main walls and roof in good structural repair and condition and that to make good all defects due to faulty materials or workmanship in the construction of the premises were held to be independent of one another. The covenant to keep the walls and roof in good structural condition was therefore unqualified and because the structural condition of the walls and roof is likely to depend on their foundations, the onus for the remedial works was firmly upon the landlord.

4.4.2 Windows

Whether windows and window frames are deemed to form part of the 'exterior' or 'outside walls' will depend upon the overall intent of the various clauses contained in the lease and the physical nature of the building.

Ball v Plummer (1879)

This was an action by a tenant of a public house against his landlord for breach of covenant to do 'outside repairs' in which it was held that 'outside repairs' included 'window repairs', the windows being part of 'the skin of the house'.

Holiday Fellowship Ltd v Hereford (1959)

A lease of a dwelling house contained a covenant by the landlord to keep the main walls and roofs in good repair and condition. The tenant covenanted to:

'... maintain and keep the demised premises and the said fixtures and fittings therein (except the roofs and main walls of the said dwelling-house ...) ... in good repair and condition ...'

The lease did not contain any covenants on the part of either the landlord or the tenant with regard to painting. A dispute arose with regard to the liability for redecoration of the windows, which in this case was defined as meaning the glass panels and the wooden framework and apparatus in which the glass is placed.

It was held that the windows were distinct from the walls in which they were inserted and not part of the main walls of the building and were therefore outside the scope of the landlord's obligation to repair.

4.4.3 Recovery of professional fees

Professional fees are recoverable under the service charge only so far as they relate to actual works, the cost of which is also recoverable.

Plough Investments Ltd v Manchester City Council (1989)

A steel-framed office building, built about 1925, showed evidence of rusting to the steel structure. The owners commissioned a full structural survey that confirmed corrosion in places. The structural engineers assumed that all the steelwork in the external wall was corroded and recommended that the steel columns and beams be exposed, which would involve the removal of the cladding, shot blasted and then enclosed in concrete to prevent any future rusting.

The lessor covenanted to keep the exterior of the building in repair and the lessees were obliged to contribute a specified proportion of the cost of carrying out repairs.

It was held that only the structural engineer's fees in relation to actual defects were recoverable and not the fees in respect of reporting on the entire steel frame.

4.5 RECTIFICATION OF INHERENT DEFECTS

Inherent defects are defects existing but not evident at the commencement of the lease and which result from defective design, construction, supervision, workmanship or materials. Whether liability for remedying an inherent defect falls within a repairing covenant will be a question of degree and whether the remedial works required involve the giving back to the landlord something different from that which was demised. There is no principle that remedying an inherent defect cannot be a repair.

Ravenseft Properties Ltd v Davstone (Holdings) Ltd (1978)

Stone cladding attached to a reinforced concrete frame of a block of flats was found to be bowing in a potentially dangerous manner. This was caused by the differential in coefficients of expansion of the materials used and the fact that the cladding was not provided with expansion joints and had not been properly tied to the frame when the block was built. Repair works carried out by the landlord consisted of tying the cladding properly to the frame and the provision of expansion joints. The provision of expansion joints would not have been standard engineering practice at the time the block was constructed.

The landlord sought recovery of the cost of the works from the tenants who contended that the remedial works resulted from an inherent defect, which could not fall within the ambit of a covenant to repair.

The Court held that the tenants were liable for the whole cost of the remedial works as there was no doctrine that want of repair due to an inherent defect could not fall within a covenant to repair and that the true test was a question of degree and whether the works were a repair or involved giving back to the landlord a wholly different thing from that which had been demised. In deciding this issue, the proportion that the cost of the works bore to the value of the whole building should be considered. The cost of inserting expansion joints was not regarded as a substantial part of the cost of the remedial works or the value of the building nor did it amount to a change in the character of the building as to take the works outside of the ambit of repair.

Smedley v Chumley & Hawkes Ltd (1982)

The landlord of a timber-framed building, located near a riverbank, covenanted:

> 'To keep the main walls and roof in good structural repair and condition throughout the term and to promptly make good all defects due to faulty materials or workmanship in the construction of the premises.'

The tenant covenanted:

> '… well and substantially to repair, maintain and keep the interior and exterior of the premises in good order and condition'.

The building was built on a concrete raft supported by piles at the river end, but not at the other. The unsupported end of the raft had sunk causing the raft to tilt.

The landlord carried out the remedial work to the foundations by driving in additional piles to support the raft. When the work was done, the premises were the same in the sense that the superstructure was the same as it had been when first built, although the foundations were different.

The tenant brought an action seeking an order that the landlord should carry out works to repair the cracking to the main walls and defects to the roof that had resulted from the earlier subsidence. The landlord pleaded that any defects in the premises were a direct consequence of the design and so outside the scope of the repairing covenant.

The landlord was held to be responsible for the further remedial works required to the walls and roof. When construing a covenant to repair, the state in which the building was in at the date of the lease and the precise terms of the lease should be looked at in order to decide if work could be termed 'repair'. The landlord's obligation to keep the main walls and roof in good structural repair and condition and that to make good all defects due to faulty materials or workmanship in the construction of the premises were held to be independent of one another. The covenant to keep the walls and roof in good structural condition was therefore unqualified and because the structural condition of the walls and roof is likely to depend on their foundations, the onus for the remedial works was firmly upon the landlord.

Elmcroft Developments Ltd v Tankersley-Sawyer (1984)

Flats suffered rising damp due to the damp-proof course having been positioned below ground level. Remedial works required the insertion of a damp-proof course by silicone injection.

The landlord covenanted to:

> '... maintain and keep the exterior of the building and the roof, the main walls, timbers and drains thereof in good and tenantable repair and condition.'

The landlord was held to be responsible for the remedial works to insert the new damp-proof course as the works required did not go beyond repair and did not involve the provision of a wholly different thing from that which was demised.

Halliard Property Co Ltd v Nicholas Clarke Investments Ltd (1984)

A tenant's repairing covenant included a jerry-built structure at the rear of the property that included a 4½ inch thick wall that was virtually unsupported apart from two brick piers. The wall collapsed and the landlord claimed that the tenant was liable to rebuild the wall in accordance with applicable building bye-laws. It was held that the reinstatement of the wall would involve handing back an edifice entirely different from the unstable and jerry-built structure of which the tenant took possession at the start of the lease.

Quick v Taff-Ely Borough Council (1986)

A house built in the early 1970s suffered severe condensation caused by a lack of insulation around the concrete window lintels, sweating from the single-glazed metal-frame windows and inadequate heating. The tenant brought an action requiring the landlord to replace the windows and face the concrete lintel under the statutory covenant to repair implied by s. 32(1) of the *Housing Act* 1961 which required the local authority, as landlord, to 'keep in repair the structure and exterior of the house'.

It was held that disrepair related to the condition of whatever had to be repaired and not to a lack of amenity and that there had to be disrepair before any question arose as to whether it would be reasonable to remedy a design fault. Since there was no evidence of damage or want of repair, the landlord was not in breach of the implied repairing covenant.

Eyre v McCracken (2000)

A tenant, granted a seven-year lease of a house which dated back to 1841, covenanted to 'put the premises in good and substantial repair and condition' and 'to well and substantially repair, maintain ... amend and keep the said premises as so intended to be put into such repair'.

The house, built without a damp-proof course, suffered damp penetration requiring the insertion of a damp-proof course in the basement. It was held that to require the tenant to insert a damp-proof course would require him to give back to the landlord a different thing from that demised to him and that did not fall within the tenant's repairing covenant.

Holding & Barnes plc v Hill House Hammond (2000)

A landlord covenanted:

'... to keep the foundations and roof in good and tenantable repair and condition and to keep the structure and exterior of the building (other than those parts comprised in the property) in good and tenantable repair and condition.'

The tenant covenanted:

'... to keep the property, including any additions after the date of this lease, in good internal repair.'

The external walls, although within the repairing obligation of the landlord, were included in the demise.

Due to the absence of a damp-proof course, the premises suffered from rising damp which had been evident virtually from the start. Because of the nature of the building and its lack of any damp-proof course from when it was constructed, it was held that the insertion of a damp-proof course was not simple repair. The cost of inserting the damp-proof course was comparatively small and the work was more intimately connected with the replacing of the floors and the repairing of the plaster on the interior walls and therefore it should be the responsibility of the tenant rather than the landlord to install a damp-proof course as part and parcel of repair works.

Daejan Properties Ltd v Bloom (2000)

The tenant of a basement garage, located beneath a courtyard serving a block of 109 flats, covenanted to pay a reasonable proportion of the charges for rebuilding, repairing and cleansing all walls, fences, drains and other 'conveniences' belonging to the premises and capable of being used by the lessee in common with the owners or occupiers of adjoining or contiguous premises.

It was held that the tenant was responsible for the cost of works to replace the asphalt membrane to the concrete slab, which comprised the roof of the garage premises and on which the forecourt and the flats were built, as this was a 'convenience' within the meaning of the lease.

However, it was also held that if it were to be established that works carried out by the lessor over the years had damaged the asphalt membrane, that the proportion of the damage should not be the responsibility of anyone other than the landlord. Conversely, in so far as any part of the damage to the membrane had been caused by incorrect laying in the first instance (i.e. inherent defect) or wear and tear over the years, this would fall under the repairing covenant for which the lessee was responsible.

4.6 RENEWAL AND REPLACEMENTS

4.6.1 Renewal

Repair is the restoration by renewal or replacement of subsidiary parts as a whole. Renewal, as distinguished from repair, is reconstruction of the entirety, meaning by the entirety not necessarily the whole but substantially the whole subject matter under discussion.

Lurcott v Wakely (1911)

A tenant of a house in London covenanted to substantially repair and keep in thorough repair and good condition the demised premises. The house was over 200 years old and shortly after the expiration of the term, the front external wall of the house was found to be a dangerous structure and the London County Council served notice requiring the wall to be rebuilt. The condition of the wall was caused by old age and the wall could not be repaired without rebuilding it. The landlord carried out the work and sought recovery of the costs from the tenant.

It was held that the tenant was liable under the covenant to reimburse the cost of taking down and rebuilding the wall. The work involved did not require the rebuilding of the whole house but a worn-out portion and, notwithstanding the wall could not have been patched or repaired and could only be rebuilt, the tenant was bound to rebuild it. The tenant was also held to be liable for the costs of rebuilding the wall below the ground in accordance with the London Building Acts.

Minja Properties Ltd v Cussins Property Group plc (1998)

The cost of replacing single-glazed windows, which had frames that were out of repair, with stronger frames and double-glazing was considered a comparatively trivial amount and quite incapable of being alteration of a kind to constitute renewal and falls outside the repairing covenant.

4.6.2   Replacement

'If the work which is done is the provision of something new ... that is, properly speaking, an improvement; but if it is only the replacement of something already there, which has become dilapidated or worn out, then albeit that it is a replacement by its modern equivalent, it comes within the category of repairs and not improvements.'

Denning LJ in *Morcom v Campbell-Johnson*

Yorkbrook Investments Ltd v Batten (1985)

A covenant on the part of the landlord to provide and maintain a good and sufficient supply of hot water and an adequate supply of heating in the hot water radiators was held to include the capital cost of replacing antiquated or unserviceable equipment which should be replaced to enable the landlord to comply with its obligation.

4.6.3   Need for replacement

A tenant would not generally be liable for the cost of replacement in the absence of any defect or disrepair to the extent requiring replacement. Similarly, a landlord may not be in breach of covenant by failing to carry out works of replacement where repair continues to be an economic option.

Murray v Birmingham City Council (1987)

There was an implied covenant under s. 32 of the *Housing Act* 1961 (now replaced by s. 11–16 of LTA 1985) for the landlord to carry out repairs to the roof. The landlord had carried out periodic repairs over time. It was held that the roof was capable of being repaired by periodic attention and had not yet reached the stage when the only practical remedial action was replacement of the roof as a whole.

Fluor Daniel Properties Ltd and others v Shortlands Investments Ltd (2001)

Leases of a modern commercial block required the landlord to maintain equipment and to provide air-conditioning and other services. The air-conditioning system was well maintained and in good working order. The landlord sought to recover £2m under the service charge provisions for upgrading the system. The landlord sought to rely on the wording of the repairing covenant, which gave the landlord express power to make reasonable additions and variations to the services.

It was held that the cost of the works was not recoverable as the service charge provisions of the lease presupposed some defect or disrepair to the equipment had to exist prior to the need for replacement. As no defect existed which required that the system to be replaced, and the proposed works were not required to maintain the service, the costs were not recoverable.

4.6.4 Replacement in anticipation of future disrepair

A landlord may be held to have acted reasonably in extending the scope of works to include replacements even though disrepair was not evident but where future disrepair was reasonably to be anticipated and the earlier procurement of the work would result in a cost saving.

Reston Ltd v Hudson (1990)

Timber window frames were found to be defective and it was more satisfactory and cheaper to replace all the timber windows at the same time than to leave it to individual tenants to do so from time to time. An issue arose as to the responsibility for replacement and whether the cost would be covered by the service charge.

The lessor covenanted to repair the windows and structures of the estate other than those for which the lessees were responsible. The service charge payable included 'cost and expenses incurred by the lessor' including the matters for which the lessor was responsible under the repairing covenants.

It was held that the replacing of the windows would be properly recoverable under the service charge.

4.6.5   Replacement with alternatives

A covenant to repair may not be complied with if the item in disrepair is replaced with something different.

Creska v Hammersmith and Fulham London Borough Council (1998)

Tenants occupied a 1960s office building with an electric under-floor heating system. The tenants held a ten-year lease and covenanted:

> '... to repair and maintain and in all respects keep in good and substantial repair and condition the interior of the Premises ... including ... all electrical heating mechanical and ventilation installations therein ...'

The system became defective and the tenant provided individual wall-mounted storage heaters. The tenant was held to be liable for carrying out repairs to the electric under-floor heating. It was not impossible or impractical to maintain the existing under-floor heating system. The tenant undertook to maintain the system in good repair, it was defective and needed repair and although the repairs would be expensive and incorporate some improvements in design this did not mean that the works ceased to be works of repair.

The tenant was not entitled to discharge its repairing obligation by the alternative method of providing individual storage heaters to replace the under-floor system.

4.7 IMPROVEMENTS

'If the work which is done is the provision of something new ... that is, properly speaking, an improvement; but if it is only the replacement of something already there, which has become dilapidated or worn out, then albeit that it is a replacement by its modern equivalent, it comes within the category of repairs and not improvements.'

Denning LJ in *Morcom v Campbell-Johnson*

4.7.1 Distinction is a question of degree

The distinction between repairs and improvements is often a question of degree and, in part, necessity. A landlord will usually have great difficulty in recovering the cost of improvements, as distinct from repairs, where this is not expressly covered in the lease.

Lister v Lane & Nesham (1893)

Lessees of a house at least 100 years old covenanted 'when and where and as often as occasion shall require, well, sufficiently, and substantially, repair, uphold, sustain, maintain ... amend and keep' the demised premises. The foundation of the house was a timber platform, which rested on a boggy or muddy soil. Prior to the end of the term rotting of the timber caused a wall to bulge out and following expiry of the lease the house was condemned as a dangerous structure and torn down.

It was held that the defect had been caused by the natural operation of time and elements upon a house, the original construction of which was faulty. The tenants covenant to repair did not extend to giving back to the landlord a different thing from that which the tenant took over or to the provision of concrete foundations, extending down to solid gravel some 17 ft below the surface of the mud.

Mullaney v Maybourne Grange (Croydon) Management Co Ltd (1986)

A landlord replaced defective old wooden-framed windows in a tenant's flat with new double-glazed windows. The landlord undertook to repair and maintain and otherwise provide services and amenities to the structure and common parts of the block. The tenant covenanted to contribute to the costs of so doing and to such further or additional costs as the defendants incurred in 'providing and maintaining additional services or amenities'. The landlord claimed installation of the new windows was a repair or that alternatively the expenditure was incurred in 'providing and maintaining additional services or amenities'. It was held that the replacement of the old windows was not a repair but a long-term improvement and although the new windows had attributes that made them desirable, they could not be regarded in the ordinary sense as an 'amenity'.

McDougall v Easington District Council (1989)

Works to remedy serious defects in the structure resulted in a house looking different upon completion; the changes were not cosmetic, the roofs, elevations and fenestration being of different materials and configuration. The outcome was a house of substantially longer life and worth nearly twice as much. It was held that the works could not be described as repairs but improvements as they gave the building a new life in a different form.

4.7.2 A repair does not cease to be a repair if it also effects an improvement

Stent v Monmouth District Council (1987)

A dwelling house which stood in an exposed location suffered constant ingress of water blown through or under the front door. The landlord carried out various remedial works over time without success, including replacement of the whole door. The problem was eventually resolved when the door was replaced with an aluminium self-sealing door unit. The tenant was awarded damages for the landlord's breach of covenant to maintain and repair the structure and exterior.

The landlord appealed on the grounds that the water penetration did not result from disrepair but to an inherent defect. It was held that: (i) the fact the door did not fulfil its function was ipso facto a defect for the purpose of the repairing covenant; (ii) the door had itself become damaged, had rotted and become out of repair; and (iii) the replacement of the wooden door with the self-sealing aluminium door was a sensible and practical repair which should have been carried out much earlier.

Sutton (Hastoe) Housing Association v Williams (1988)

The tenant of a block of flats covenanted to pay a service charge being a proportion of the costs of various matters including within the lessor's covenants as follows:

'5(1)(a)(i) maintaining, repairing, renewing and in all ways keeping in good condition the Block …

5(1)(a)(viii) carrying out such works and providing such additional works and services as may be considered necessary by the lessor in its absolute discretion from time to time.'

The lease made reference to a Schedule of Condition and a Schedule of Repairs to the structure anticipated during the next ten years that stated:

'External timber elements will need to be renewed during the next ten years. This includes windows, timber cladding to fascias and garage doors.'

Wet rot in the woodwork of windows had caused leaks and had required constant repairs.

The Housing Association decided to replace the old single-glazed wooden windows with double-glazed uPVC windows.

The tenant appealed an earlier county court judgment that did not distinguish between repairs and improvements. The county court judge's finding was upheld that there was no need to as the replacement of the windows, whether amounting to repair or including an element of improvement, was covered by the wording under 5(1)(a) of the lease, whether under subsection (i) or (viii).

Although not disagreeing with the decision in *Mullaney v Maybourne Grange* above, because of the terms of the lease, the question of whether the work could be both repair and improvement did not arise.

Minja Properties Ltd v Cussins Property Group plc (1998)

The cost of replacing single-glazed windows, which had frames that were out of repair, with stronger frames and double-glazing was considered a comparatively trivial amount and quite incapable of being alteration of a kind to constitute renewal and falls outside the repairing covenant.

Wandsworth London Borough Council v Griffin (2000)

A block of flats were constructed with flat roofs and had metal-framed windows which were in disrepair. Wandsworth London Borough Council replaced the flat roofs with pitched roofs and the windows with uPVC double-glazed units. It was held that within the meaning of the Council's repairing obligations, the works constituted repair as they were cheaper than the alternatives, taking into account both initial and future costs and that the decision to replace the flat roofs with pitched roofs and the windows with uPVC double-glazed units was a reasonable one.

Gibson Investments Ltd v Chesterton plc (No 2) 2003

A lease of an office block let for a term of 33 years and granted in 1979 contained tenants covenanted to maintain the air-conditioning apparatus in good working order and condition.

The system was out of repair and it was agreed that the tenant was liable for the replacement of the defective system. The case centred on the issue of whether the replacement of the defective air-conditioning system would be an improvement or a repair. This was particularly relevant for the rent review, where an improvement would be disregarded but a repair would not.

The new system was to be located in the ceiling void, which would release additional floor space as the original system was laid in casing round the perimeter at floor level. The landlord argued that the new system would be an alteration, for which landlord's consent would be required, and which the landlord would be entitled to require to be reinstated at the end of the term.

It was held that neither the relocation of the pipe work in the ceiling nor the removal of the casings was necessary for the tenant to discharge his repairing obligation and accordingly the proposed works amounted to an improvement.

4.7.3 Recovery of the cost of improvements which reduce future service charge costs

The courts have taken a more common-sense approach in allowing the landlord to recover the cost of improvements, the effect of which would be to reduce the long-term cost of repairs and thereby have a positive effect upon future service charge costs.

Postel Properties Ltd v Boots the Chemist (1996)

The landlord carried out repairs to low-level roofs and upper windows of a large shopping centre. The flat low-level roofs, which were constructed in 1975 and 1976 with a maximum life expectancy of 20 years, were re-covered under a phased programme. The tenants argued that the replacement of the roof covering was premature and the specification was increased to a point where there was an irrecoverable excess, and that the work to the windows was due to rust which could have been contained with timeous maintenance.

It was held that the repairs to the roof were repairs that a reasonably minded building owner might undertake and they did not amount to giving back to the landlord something different from that which existed before. It was reasonable to commence them when the landlord did, notwithstanding that some parts had not yet failed. However, the landlord was not able to recover the cost of priming the roof troughs, as this served no useful purpose, as they showed no evidence of deterioration. The works to the windows and cladding were repairs, and, in so far as the landlord may have been guilty of delay in carrying out such works, that was more than balanced by the saved costs of earlier repainting.

4.8 CAPITAL EXPENDITURE

It is a commonly held misconception that 'capital' expenditure relates to the improvement of the landlord's asset and is not, in the absence of very clear wording, a cost that should generally be recovered through the service charge. However, the definition of what constitutes revenue or capital expenditure is one laid down by Her Majesty's Revenue and Customs. In the context of property, the replacement of an element of a building, whilst falling within the definition of 'repair' might, in certain circumstances, be treated as capital expenditure for the purposes of the landlord's tax computation. The costs recoverable under a service charge are not therefore, per se, limited to revenue expenditure only.

Yorkbrook Investments Ltd v Batten (1985)

A covenant on the part of the landlord to provide and maintain a good and sufficient supply of hot water and an adequate supply of heating in the hot water radiators was held to include the capital cost of replacing antiquated or unserviceable equipment which should be replaced to enable the landlord to comply with its obligation.

Sun Alliance and London Assurance Co Ltd v British Railways Board (1989)

Leases granted in respect of a building provided that the tenants were responsible for external window cleaning. The landlord had actually carried out this service as it was not possible for the tenant to carry out the cleaning in compliance with the *Health and Safety at Work Act* 1974. The tenants had accepted the position and had reimbursed the landlord his costs incurred in cleaning the exterior of the windows over a number of years. The landlord replaced a 'ramshackle' arrangement for gaining access to the windows with a modern automated system requiring additional works to strengthen the roof.

The tenant covenanted to contribute towards:

'The cost of providing such other services as the lessor shall consider ought properly and reasonably to be provided for the benefit of the building, or for the proper maintenance and servicing of any part or parts thereof.'

It was held that the landlord had 'properly and reasonably' considered that the improved window-cleaning service was one that ought to be provided for the benefit of the building and its proper maintenance and servicing. Notwithstanding the fairly heavy capital cost involved in the new installation, the landlord was entitled to recover the contributions demanded from the tenants.

The landlord's position was, however, helped as recovery of the total cost of the new window-cleaning cradle had not been sought. The new system was clearly an upgrading or improvement from the existing system. To the extent that the new system was a replacement of the old, the cost was recoverable although the proportion of the landlord's costs attributable to the upgrading of the system was not claimed.

Lloyds Bank plc v Bowker Orford (1992)

The tenant covenanted to pay a service charge being the due proportion of the total cost to the lessor of providing, amongst other things, a lift service, a caretaker, security, cleaning and lighting of common parts, cleaning and lighting of lavatories, constant hot water, and 'any other beneficial services which may properly be provided by the lessee'.

The landlord sought to recover the costs of capital as opposed to revenue expenditure in respect of plant and equipment providing hot water to the lavatories, the heating of the common parts and the provision of lifts. It was held that the specified services recoverable under the lease were not limited to revenue items and the landlord was entitled to recover the 'total cost' of providing the services.

5
Sinking funds, reserve funds and depreciation

Sinking funds

A sinking fund is a replacement fund by which the landlord aims to build up over time a fund to pay for repair and replacement of major items of plant and equipment. The fund would usually be accumulated over the anticipated life of the item and may often therefore include costs that might be expended beyond the term of the occupation leases.

Reserve funds

A reserve fund is a fund built up to equalise expenditure in respect of regularly recurring service items so as to avoid fluctuations in the amount of service charge payable each year.

Some leases make provision for the service charge to include a sum or sums (often at the landlord's discretion) being a proportion of any costs and outgoings which are of a periodically recurring nature or to provide for anticipated future expenditure which the landlord properly considers may be necessary during the term.

Hitherto, the distinction between reserve funds and sinking funds has become confused although recent case law has served to clarify matters (see below).

Depreciation

Fixed assets have a finite useful economic life, which is the period over which its owner will derive economic benefit from its use.

Depreciation is the measure of the wearing out, consumption or other reduction in life of the asset. The purpose of a depreciation charge against income in the financial statements of enterprises using such assets is to reflect that part of the costs to the enterprise.

A depreciation provision within the service charge clause of a lease would enable the landlord to include an amount to reflect this 'cost' of the annual depreciation of plant and equipment.

From the tenants' perspective therefore depreciation 'fund' is a misnomer as monies received by the landlord would not have to be set aside and accumulated to defray the cost of future expenditure (although a landlord may well choose to do so) and is broadly the landlord's to do with as he will.

5.1 OWNERSHIP OF THE FUNDS

Section 18 of LTA 1985 places a statutory requirement for the investment of monies received in respect of residential dwellings as trust funds. CLRA 2002 includes a new s. 42 of LTA 1987 which provides that service charge contributions (including sinking fund contributions) in respect of residential dwellings are to be held on trust in a designated account with a relevant institution.

5.1.1 Implied or constructed trust

Monies held in a reserve or sinking fund might be treated as if they form part of an implied or constructed trust. If the landlord were to sell the entire property it would not be for the landlord to retain the reserve fund but to transfer the monies held to the new owner.

Re Kayford Ltd (1975)

This case involved a company that carried out a mail-order business where customers either paid the full purchase price or a deposit when ordering goods. The company experienced financial difficulties and, having taken advice on how their customers might be protected in the event of the company becoming insolvent, opened a bank account to be called 'Customers' Trust Deposit Account'. In the liquidation proceedings that followed, the question arose whether the sums paid into the account were held on trust for those who had sent the money or whether they formed part of the general assets of the company.

It was held that in the circumstances a trust had been created. In giving judgment, Megarry J stated:

'... it seems to me that where money in advance is being paid to a company in return for the future supply of goods or services, it is an entirely proper and honourable thing for a company to do what this company did, on skilled advice, namely, to start to pay the money into a trust account as soon as there began to be doubts as to the company's ability to fulfil its obligations to deliver the goods or services. I wish that, sitting in this court, I had heard of this occurring more frequently; and can only hope that I shall hear more of it in the future.'

Re Chelsea Cloisters (in liquidation) (1981)

A landlord of a block of flats entered into an agreement to grant an intermediate under-lease to a company formed to manage the block. The standard furnished tenancy agreements provided for each tenant to pay a deposit against any sum that might be due from the tenant at the end of the tenancy and dilapidations. Any balance was to be credited to the tenant at the termination of the tenancy.

The company got into financial difficulties and an accountant, appointed to supervise the running of the company, opened a separate bank account into which the deposits received were paid.

The company went into voluntary liquidation and it was subsequently held that the deposit monies should not be dealt with as money generally available to the creditors of the company but should go to the landlord in trust for the tenants. Although it was unlikely a trust was created in respect of the deposits from the beginning, since the deposits were made contractually with an obligation to repay the whole or some lesser sum, the nature of the transaction was inevitably such as to create a trust under the original tenancy agreements. The company could only retain the money as agents for the landlord who were thus entitled to the whole fund together with interest accrued upon it.

5.1.2   Funds held 'in reserve' belong to the tenants

Where a lease makes provision for the service charge to include a sum or sums (often at the landlord's discretion) being a proportion of any costs and outgoings which are of a periodically recurring nature, or to provide for anticipated future expenditure which the landlord properly considers may be necessary during the term, the funds accumulated are to be treated as intended to even out demands on tenants during the course of the lease.

If the lease does not make any express provision as to how any surplus should be dealt with, any money remaining unspent at the end of the lease should belong to the tenants.

Brown's Operating System Services Ltd v Southwark Roman Catholic Diocesan Corporation (2007)

The tenant covenanted to pay a service charge being a contribution towards the 'Total service Cost' to include 'such sum as the landlord shall ... think fit as being a reasonable provision for expenditure likely to be incurred in the future in connection with the matters mentioned in this Schedule' (the Schedule setting out the services to be provided).

The lease also provided that any excess arising from the tenant's on-account payments could be retained to cover any deficiency in the following year and that the landlord would only be entitled to demand further sums for the provision of services if the money held by the landlord in reserve were insufficient to meet any shortfall.

The landlord's policy was to build up a surplus from the annual charges to cover future expenditure and over a period of ten years a substantial sum had built up. The tenant thought that the money was being retained to his credit and that the size of the sum accumulated by 2002 entitled him to a service charge 'holiday'. When the landlord refused, the tenant exercised an option to break and withheld payment of the last two quarters' service charge, totalling almost £10,000, for which the landlord sued. The tenant counterclaimed seeking recovery of sums held by the landlord as surplus.

The landlord argued that the service charge provision of the lease entitled it to create a reserve fund to defray its future liabilities as landlord. However, the Court of Appeal held that the lease permitted the landlord to include in the total service cost a reasonable sum for future repairs but did not provide for the creation of a reserve fund and that nowhere in the lease does the expression 'reserve fund' appear.

The monies were intended to even out demands on tenants during the course of the lease; and that the tenant's obligation was limited to contribute to works reasonably required during the term, but not in respect of works that might be required after termination of the lease.

The leases did not make any express provision as to how any surplus should be dealt with at the end of the lease and therefore any money remaining unspent at the end of the lease should belong to the tenants.

5.1.3 Landlord's 'own' depreciation charges

Where the service charge includes for the landlord to recover depreciation, it has been held that the money collected from tenants belongs to the landlord absolutely and the payments should not be treated as being made on account of future expenditure. Even though the landlord has an obligation to maintain and repair the equipment which might require the landlord to replace the equipment when required, the fact that the need to replace the equipment did not arise during the term of the lease is immaterial.

Secretary of State for the Environment v Possfund (North West) Ltd (1997)

The tenant was obliged to pay a depreciation allowance in respect of the cost of maintaining and replacing, amongst other things, fixtures and fittings, and in particular the air-conditioning plant. Under the lease, the landlord covenanted to maintain the air-conditioning plant. The sums paid over the term of the lease in respect of the depreciation allowance had not been expended by the landlord on replacing the air-conditioning plant by the date the tenants lease had expired. The tenant claimed repayment of the fund.

However, it was held that it was irrelevant that the landlord did not spend the fund on replacing the air-conditioning during the period of the tenancy. Once the payments were made they became the landlord's absolute property. The commercial reality was that the life of the air-conditioning might not have had a life coterminous with the leases. The cost to the landlord of running the air-conditioning included its depreciation, which the tenant had agreed to indemnify. One factor against the tenant's contention was the absence of any machinery in the leases for the repayment of the fund.

Note: It is the author's opinion that this case creates further confusion with regard to the definition between sinking funds and the inappropriately named depreciation fund. Whilst I would concur with the judge's ruling, I cannot understand the point made with reference to the lack of a provision for repayment of the fund as, in charging 'depreciation' as a *cost* to the landlord, no 'fund' would (or should) accumulate.

5.2 RESERVE FUNDS

Landlord and Tenant Act 1985

Section 19(2) of LTA 1985 provides that advance payments (including contributions to reserve funds) must be reasonable.

Commonhold and Leasehold Reform Act 2002

CLRA 2002 introduces a new s. 42 to LTA 1987 requiring all interim payments and other payments (i.e. sinking funds) to be held in designated accounts at a relevant financial institution.

5.2.1 Contributions towards sinking or reserve funds should be in respect of specific items

A landlord is only entitled to apply monies to a reserve or sinking fund which are fair and reasonable and in respect of specifically identified expenditure for which the fund was created or intended rather than other, unidentified, future expenses. In the absence of provision in the lease, a landlord cannot arbitrarily transfer a surplus in the on-account service charge payments made by tenants to a reserve or sinking fund.

St Mary's Mansions Ltd v Limegate Investment Co Ltd (2002)

Leases of a block of flats provided for the service charge to include, inter alia:

> '… a sum or sums by way of reasonable provision for anticipated expenditure in respect … as the lessor or its accountants or managing agents (as the case may be) may in their discretion allocate to the year in question as being fair and reasonable in the circumstances.'

In addition to sums relating to specific major projects, surplus payments into the service charge account were also transferred to the reserve fund. The reserve fund held a figure approaching £1m.

It was held that, whilst the leases entitled the landlord to establish and maintain a reserve fund, the landlord was entitled to apply to the reserve fund only such reasonable expenses, outgoings and other expenditure that were of a periodically recurring nature, including the provision for anticipated expenditure provided that: (i) the allocation to the year in question was fair and reasonable; and (ii) that a sufficient description of the future project and the amount set aside for it was provided.

Any sums held in the reserve fund for periodically recurring expenditure, properly allocated and certified would not be repayable to the occupational lessees but any surplus in the service charge account was to be repaid or credited to the individual lessees at the end of each year and should not be transferred to the reserve fund.

5.2.2 Tenants' contributions to reserve or sinking funds should not exceed a sum reasonably required to meet the anticipated future liabilities

Landlords, in establishing a reserve or sinking fund, should only seek to build up a fund sufficient to meet the reasonably anticipated cost of future major repairs or replacements for which the fund is intended. When incurring expenditure, the landlord should have regard to funds already accumulated in a reserve or sinking fund before seeking separate reimbursement from tenants.

Fluor Daniel Properties Ltd and others v Shortlands Investments Ltd (2001)

Leases of a modern commercial block required the landlord to maintain equipment and to provide air-conditioning and other services. The leases also provided for the landlord to establish a reserve fund for anticipated future expenditure. The monies accumulated in the reserve fund amounted to some £850,000 by the end of the 1998–99 service charge year.

The landlord sought to recover in excess of £2m under the service charge provisions for upgrading the air-conditioning system and other works and further proposed covering the cost by means of:

(1) an additional reserve fund contribution, included in the audited service charge account for the year ending 30 April 1998, of £750,000 (the effect of which was to increase the overall reserve fund contribution for that year to £800,000 as the landlord had only budgeted £50,000);

(2) a £750,000 provision in the estimate of the repairs within the service charge budget for the year then current; and

(3) a contribution of £500,000 from the reserve fund, over and above the £750,000 to be added to it.

The service charge budget for the year then current also provided for a reserve fund contribution of £150,000. This would have the effect of reducing the net outflow from the reserve fund to £350,000

It was held that seeking to increase the amount of the previous year's service charge expenditure by retrospectively increasing the amount of the tenants' reserve fund contribution was a ploy to recover, in advance of any expenditure being incurred, as much as possible of the anticipated costs of the works without going through the correct machinery for increases in service charge demands as provided by the lease.

It was therefore concluded that: (i) the landlord was not entitled retrospectively to increase the contribution to the reserve fund; and (ii) the landlord ought to have looked to the reserve fund to cover the whole cost (so far as it could) of works which it was agreed would fall to be undertaken at the tenants' expense.

As to the inclusion of £150,000 as a contribution to the reserve fund in 1998–99, this represented a substantial increase in the reserve fund contribution included in the previous years and was held to be excessive as the balance remaining in the fund would have far exceeded the anticipated funds required in order to meet the likely cost of major repairs and renewals.

6
Fees and associated costs

Most service charges provide for the landlord to recover the costs of administering the building and the service charge. However, there are often fees incurred in addition to the management charge. Frequently, this might include professional building surveyors' or architects' fees for the tendering and supervision of major works contracts, specialist fees in obtaining advice on such matters as health and safety, etc.

6.1 MANAGEMENT FEES

Landlord and Tenant Act 1985, s. 19

Management fees charged to residential dwellings will be subject to the reasonableness tests under s. 19 of LTA 1985. Where a lease provides for a landlord to recover in-house management charges, these will also be subject to the reasonable test under s. 18(3)(a) which includes overheads in the definition of 'costs'.

6.1.1 Lease must include specific provision

Unless the managing agent's fees are expressly provided for in the service charge provisions, the landlord may not be able to recover them.

Parkside Knightsbridge Ltd v Horwitz (1983)

The amount claimed by the landlord in respect of supervision and management services carried out by a parent company, as agent for the landlord company, was held to be a proper charge.

Embassy Court Residents' Association Ltd v Lipman (1984)

The Court held there should be an implied term that, to give business efficacy to the leases, a residents' association could incur proper expenditure to carry out the functions imposed on it, which included the payment of management fees to managing agents.

6.1.2 Management fees included in 'total cost' of providing services

If the lease provides for the landlord to recover the 'total cost' of providing services this would include the cost of employing agents for the management and administration of the services.

Lloyds Bank plc v Bowker Orford (1992)

The tenant covenanted to pay a service charge comprising 'the total cost to the lessor' in providing the specified services and 'defraying the costs and expenses relating and incidental to such services'.

The landlord sought to recover the costs of employing managing agents to carry out and provide the specified services.

It was held that the landlord was entitled to recover the cost of employing managing agents to organise and supervise the provision of services.

6.1.3 Management fees are distinct from professional fees

Where a lease provides for the recovery of a management fee and which is limited to a percentage of the aggregate of the service charge expenditure, the cap would not extend to professional fees.

Church Commissioners for England v Metroland Ltd (1996)

A lease included within the service charge provisions:

> '... the administrative costs to the Landlord of managing the Development including the proper fees and expenses of any management company and/or consultant or

professional employed or engaged by the Landlord ... and where management is undertaken directly by the landlord a reasonable fee there from.'

The lease also provided that:

'The aggregate charge made to the tenants of the Development in respect of the costs to the landlord of any management company employed or engaged in it cannot exceed 6 per cent of the remaining annual expenditure.'

It was held that the limitation was restricted to the costs of the landlord and of any management company employed or engaged by it. Both these costs are service charges, but together they are subject to the capping. Professional advisers are on a different basis. If they are consultants or professionals engaged exclusively in consultancy and advisory services, their fees are part of the administration costs of the landlord but are not subject to the capping. Such costs are costs *to* the landlord not *of* the landlord.

6.1.4 Recovery of scale fees

Where a lease makes reference to the management fees calculated in accordance with a scale fee that is subsequently abolished, the courts will give weight to the purpose of a clause and will interpret the provisions of the lease accordingly.

Thames Side Properties Ltd v Brixton Estates plc (1997)

Leases contained provision for payment by the tenants of the landlord's managing agent's fees for managing the building calculated in accordance with the scale laid down by RICS. Since the date of the grant of the lease, RICS abrogated the scale following comment made by the Monopolies Commission that such scales operated against public interest.

The landlord engaged a subsidiary as managing agent and sought to charge the fee recommended by the scale at the date of the grant of the lease which was considerably in excess of the reasonable fee for such services.

It was held that on the true construction of the clause the landlord was not bound to pay the managing agent the scale fee; they could pay more (in which case the landlord would make a loss) or less (in which case the landlord would make a profit). But the expectation plainly is that there will be no profit or loss. The clause did not expressly provide for the fees to be calculated in accordance with the scale laid down 'from time to time' nor did it make any provision for abrogation of the scale. In view of the purpose of the clause, the fact that the leases were for a substantial period of years, and that the scale was obviously liable to be amended from time to time, the business purpose and language of the clause required that reference to the scale be read as reference to the scale from time to time in force.

As to the quantum of fees payable, given that the scale had been abolished, the purpose of the clause was to entitle the landlord to reimbursement of what is the reasonable cost of obtaining the services. As the scale fee was no longer available, the fee should be calculated as the fee for managing the building after arm's length negotiations between the landlord and a prospective managing agent.

6.1.5 In the absence of wording to the contrary, management fees should reflect the actual costs of managing the services

St Modwen Developments (Edmonton) Ltd v Tesco Stores Ltd (2007)

St Modwen acquired the freehold reversion to premises in the Edmonton Green shopping centre from the borough council. The landlord brought proceedings to establish its entitlement to: (i) service charges certified by its finance director in place of the borough treasurer; (ii) a contribution to the cost of refuse collection for other tenants, in circumstances where the tenant disposed of its own refuse; and (iii) a 10 per cent management fee.

It was held that although the addition of 10 per cent for management fees was a common modern practice, and that in many other cases the parties would be happy to accept the adding of a general percentage as a rough and ready approach, the landlord's right to charge such fees was determined by the terms of the lease.

The judge commented that 10 per cent as a percentage has no magic value and that the landlord was not entitled to a figure of 10 per cent taken, so to speak, from the air in the absence of any investigation into the cost of providing the services in question.

6.2   IN-HOUSE MANAGEMENT CHARGES

If a lease provides for the cost of employing external managing agents, but does not make provision for the alternative of allowing the landlord to charge for providing his own internal staff, the lease would not usually allow the landlord to recover such costs.

Cleve House Properties Ltd v Schidlof (1980)

It was held that the landlords were not entitled to claim a management fee where the landlords' directors in fact performed the management functions gratuitously, so that no actual expenditure was incurred.

Parkside Knightsbridge Ltd v Horwitz (1983)

The amount claimed by the landlords in respect of supervision and management services carried out by a parent company, as agent for the landlord company, was held to be a proper charge.

6.3   APPOINTMENT OF MANAGING AGENTS

A management agent does not require to have a formal professional qualification but must be a separate legal entity from the landlords.

New Pinehurst Residents Association (Cambridge) Ltd v Silow (1988)

A lease, which was originally granted by a development company, provided for the appointment and duties of managing agents, who were to act as experts and not arbitrators.

The tenants' association appointed a committee of tenant shareholders as managing agents and the decision before the Court was whether the appointment of the committee was a proper appointment from the point of view of independence and expertise.

The Court of Appeal upheld the earlier county court decision that although not professional surveyors or estate agents, the members of the committee had experience of worldly affairs and in some cases of actual property management and even though they were themselves tenants they were separate legal persons from the landlords and had some independence of mind and sufficient expertise to discharge their duties.

6.4 MANAGEMENT COMPANIES

6.4.1 Management companies should not be a sham

A landlord may set up a management company in order to manage the property on his behalf as it may be convenient for the landlord not to carry out the services himself or he may not want the responsibility. A management company may be landlord controlled (commercial) or tenant controlled (residential).

Skilleter v Charles (1992)

Leases of a block of flats provided that there could be charged to the maintenance fund certain costs and expenses, including the cost of employing a managing agent and all other legal and proper costs incurred.

It was held that the management fees payable to a company formed by the landlord to manage the block and other properties were recoverable. The lease expressly permitted the employment of a manager and for that manager to be paid. There is no reason why a landlord should not employ a company and charge therefore, even if he owned the company, provided that it was not a complete sham.

6.4.2 Landlord should covenant to procure performance by the management company

Where a landlord establishes a management company to carry out the services, the tenant should insist on the lease including a covenant that the landlord will provide the services or procure performance by the management company. Otherwise, a landlord may not be liable for the non-performance of the services by the management company.

Hafton Properties Ltd v Camp (1994)

The tenant covenanted with the lessor and the management company incorporated to manage the building and provide services to the tenants to pay a maintenance charge being a specific proportion of the management company's costs expended in respect of certain items. The management company covenanted to carry out repairs and maintenance.

It was held that a term could not be implied that the lessor would observe the covenants for repair and maintenance on behalf of the management company. The more comprehensive a code in the lease (for the carrying out of repairs and the payment of them) the less room there is for the implication of a term.

6.5 OTHER PROFESSIONAL FEES

6.5.1 Professional fees included in 'total cost' of providing services

Whether the service charge provisions do not specifically make reference to the cost of management fees, the costs of professional fees incurred for the specification, tendering and supervision of repair works will often be recoverable where the service charge is expressed to cover the 'total costs or expenses incurred by the landlord'.

Lloyds Bank plc v Bowker Orford (1992)

The tenant covenanted to pay a service charge comprising 'the total cost to the lessor' in providing the specified services and 'defraying the costs and expenses relating and incidental to such services'.

The landlord sought to recover the costs of employing managing agents to carry out and provide the specified services.

The landlord was entitled to recover the cost of employing managing agents to organise and supervise the provision of the services.

6.5.2 Professional fees must relate to recoverable expenditure

Professional fees must relate to works or services actually recoverable. Fees incurred in respect of items that extend beyond the items recoverable under the service charge provisions may not be recoverable.

Plough Investments Ltd v Manchester City Council (1989)

A steel-framed office building, built in about 1925, showed evidence of rusting to the steel structure. The owners commissioned a full structural survey that confirmed corrosion in places. The structural engineers assumed that all the steelwork in the external wall was corroded and recommended that the steel columns and beams be exposed, which would involve the removal of the cladding, shot blasted and then enclosed in concrete to prevent any future rusting.

The lessor covenanted to keep the exterior of the building in repair and the lessees were obliged to contribute a specified proportion of the cost of carrying out repairs.

It was held that only the structural engineer's fees in relation to actual defects were recoverable and not the fees in respect of reporting on the entire steel frame.

Holding and Management Ltd v Property Holding and Investment Trust plc (1989)

Substantial remedial works were required to a block of flats. The Court determined that costs of scaffolding and some, but not all, of the cost of engineer's fees, legal fees and disbursements were recoverable.

The work arose following discovery of defects to the external walls of a 12-storey block of flats constructed of reinforced concrete with brickwork cladding. Various schemes were put forward for remedying the defects, one of which was an elaborate scheme, in excess of £1m, to remove the entire brickwork 'skin' that went beyond repair. A subsequent scheme of works costing approximately £250,000 was agreed.

The Court disallowed the engineer's fees, legal fees and disbursements incurred for the promotion of the elaborate scheme. The maintenance trustees' own costs were also found not to be recoverable as the trustees had taken an adversarial course.

6.6 COSTS OF ENFORCING TENANT COVENANTS

A service charge would not usually include costs for enforcing tenants' covenants or other matters between an owner and an individual occupier, for instance: enforcement of covenants for collection of rent, costs of letting units, consents for assignments, sub-letting, alterations, rent reviews, etc.

6.6.1 Rent collection is not administration of the building

The cost of debt collection and rent arrears would not fall within the definition of administration of the building.

Sella House Ltd v Mears (1989)

A lease entitled the landlord to recover 'fees of agents or other persons managing the building including the cost of computing and collecting rents and service charges' and the cost of 'employing professional persons necessary or desirable for the proper maintenance, safety and administration of the building'. It was held that the landlord was not able to recover the costs of lawyers' fees incurred in recovering rent and the service charge.

6.6.2 Cost of forfeiture proceedings

Legal costs incurred in enforcing tenants' covenants relating to the service charge may be recoverable as a cost of management although this would not extend to the cost of forfeiting a defaulting tenant's lease.

Reston v Hudson (1990)

Timber window frames were found to be defective and it was more satisfactory and cheaper to replace all the timber windows at the same time than to leave it to individual tenants to do so from time to time. An issue arose as to the responsibility for replacement and whether the cost would be covered by the service charge.

The lessor covenanted to repair the windows and structures of the estate other than those for which the lessees were responsible. The lessor sought to first circularise the tenants to inform them of the proposals and, having received certain objections from some tenants, took the precaution of going to the Court for an appropriate declaration.

Under the lease, there could be included in the service charge 'the cost of management of the estate' and 'all outgoings, costs and expenses whatsoever which the lessor may reasonably incur in the discharge of its obligations under … the lease and not otherwise hereinbefore specifically mentioned'. It was held that this included not just the cost of actual works of repair, but other matters which came within the lessor's covenants. Where the lessor sought a declaration from the Court, due to the difficulties in interpreting the lease, it was held that the lessor had reasonably incurred the costs of the application, which could be included within the service charge.

Morgan v Stainer (1993)

Tenants were required to contribute to a specified sum for the carrying out of maintenance. Under para. 5(b) of the standard form of lease, the tenants were also obliged 'to pay all legal and other costs that may be incurred by the landlord in obtaining the payment of the maintenance contribution from any tenant in the building'.

Some years prior, the tenants had issued proceedings against the landlord on a related matter, which were settled on terms including that the landlord paid the tenants' costs. The landlord then sought to recover the cost incurred in relation to the earlier proceedings under para. 5(b).

It was held that the cost were not 'costs incurred in obtaining the payment of the maintenance contribution' but costs incurred in resisting the tenants' proceedings. The agreement reached was also clear that the landlord was to pay the tenants' costs and the tenants could not then be liable to pay through another route.

Moreover, applying established principles the 'legal and other costs' had to be reasonably and properly incurred, not only with regard to their amount but also with regard to their nature. As the landlord had agreed to pay the tenants' costs, there had to be a presumption that the sums claimed were not reasonable or properly incurred.

St Mary's Mansions Ltd v Limegate Investment Co Ltd (2002)

A lease entitled the landlord to recover the costs of 'all other services which the lessor may at its absolute discretion provide' and the reasonable and proper fees for general management of the property. It was held that the wording of the lease did not entitle the landlord to recover legal costs of proceedings to recover arrears.

6.6.3 Landlord's legal costs

If a landlord loses legal proceedings and is ordered to pay costs, he cannot recover them against the service charge provisions.

Iperion Investments Corporation v Broadwalk House Residents Ltd (1994)

All costs properly incurred in the proper and reasonable management of the property could be taken into account in calculating the service charge and would include the cost of unsuccessful proceedings properly brought in managing the property.

A tenant who had been substantially successful in litigation against his landlord and who has an award of costs in his favour should not find himself having to pay the landlord's costs through the service charge.

However, if the landlord's conduct is considered to have been reprehensible even though judgment is awarded in his favour, it is just and equitable for the court to exercise discretion and order that costs be excluded when calculating the service charge.

The cost of proceedings in opposing a tenant's application to replace a landlord's defaulting manager with another manager cannot be recovered from tenants generally as a service charge incurred in connection with management.

Schilling v Canary Riverside Developments PTE Ltd (2005)

Tenants sought to appoint a manager of a mixed-use estate under s. 34 of LTA 1987. The application was refused and the landlord subsequently claimed their costs of the proceedings as a service charge item.

It was held that the landlord had not established a contractual right under the under-leases to have their tribunal costs paid as a service charge. The service charge provisions were to be construed restrictively and in order for the landlord to be entitled to recover such costs from the tenants it was necessary for the contractual provisions to contain clear terms entitling it to do so.

7
Funding and interest on borrowed funds

Interim or 'on-account' payments made by tenants would usually provide the landlord with sufficient funds to defray the costs of providing the services and in complying with the landlord's service charge obligations under the lease. Where the lease does not provide a mechanism for the collection of interim payments on account, or the interim payments are insufficient to meet the payments due, the landlord may have to expend his own money or borrow externally to finance the provision of the services.

The extent to which the landlord will be able to demand payment 'on-account' or to recover actual or notional interest will be dependent upon the wording of the lease.

7.1 LANDLORD'S OBLIGATION IRRESPECTIVE OF FUNDING

A lack of funds would not absolve the landlord from responsibility to provide services pursuant to the covenants contained in the lease.

Marenco v Jacramel (1964)

A landlord covenanted to keep and maintain the exterior of a block of 12 flats in good repair and condition and properly maintained including the entrances, passageways, staircases, fences, etc.

The tenant covenanted to pay a proportion of the costs of insuring the building and a fair proportion of the cost of keeping clean and lighting the entrance and staircase and to contribute a rateable or due proportion of the expense of making, repairing, maintaining, etc. the exterior of the building, fences, etc.

The tenant served notice on the landlords requiring them to carry out various works for which they were responsible. The landlords were not however prepared to carry out the works until the other lessees of the block had contributed to the cost of previous works carried out and given security for future contributions.

It was held that the landlords were in breach of covenant and that the fact that other tenants had not paid their service charges did not alter the landlords' obligation to comply with their covenants.

Francis v Cowcliffe (1977)

A landlord covenanted to provide various services including the supply and maintenance of a lift. A hydraulic lift required repairs and could not be operated due to a lack of supply of water under pressure. The landlords got into financial difficulties and were insolvent. They obtained expert advice and bought another lift but could not have it installed due to a lack of funds. The tenant brought an action seeking an order for specific performance of the covenant. The order for specific performance was granted even though the inevitable outcome would result in the landlords being wound up.

Yorkbrook Investments v Batten (1985)

The landlord covenanted to provide and maintain a good, sufficient and constant supply of hot and cold water to the building and also an adequate supply of heating in the radiators 'subject to the Lessee paying the maintenance contribution'. It was held that this was not a condition precedent to any liability on the part of the landlord to provide hot water and central heating.

However, if a tenant wilfully withholds payment which itself causes the landlord's inability to perform its obligations, the position will be different.

Bluestorm Ltd v Portvale Holdings Ltd (2004)

A subsidiary company of Portvale was the freeholder of a block of flats who also acquired the leasehold interest in 35 out of a total of 57 flats in the block. The building was in a poor state of repair. Two tenants successfully obtained judgment against the landlord for damages for breaches of the landlord's repairing covenants. The landlord company was then dissolved and the freehold was acquired by Bluestorm, a company controlled by the tenants of the 22 flats unconnected with Portvale.

Portvale then gave notice to Bluestorm alleging breach of the landlord's repairing covenants and withheld payment of the rent and service charge. Bluestorm commenced proceedings for arrears of rent and service charge; Portvale counterclaimed for damages for the dilapidated state of the building.

The county court gave judgment to Bluestorm which was upheld at the Court of Appeal. The decision, on the face of it, appears to be contrary to the decision in *Yorkbrook Investments v Batten* (1985), however, the court found that the tenant's refusal to pay resulted in the landlord's inability to perform and whilst the claim might be equitable in its origins and nature, Portvale should be denied equitable relief as the dilapidated state of the building was originally due to Portvale's subsidiary company's original neglect of the building prior to the acquisition by Bluestorm.

7.2 INTERIM OR ON-ACCOUNT CONTRIBUTIONS FROM TENANTS

Landlord and Tenant Act 1985

Section 19(2) of LTA 1985 provides that advance payments must be reasonable.]

Landlord and Tenant Act 1987

Section 42 of LTA 1987 provides that advance payments received by a landlord are to be held on trust.

Commonhold and Leasehold Reform Act 2002

CLRA 2002 introduces a new s. 42 to LTA 1987 requiring all interim payments and other payments (i.e. sinking funds) to be held in designated accounts at a relevant financial institution.

7.2.1 The provision of a landlord's estimate as a necessary precondition

If a lease provides for a tenant to make interim or on-account service charge payments based on the landlord's estimate, the tenant will have no liability to make such payments in the absence of such estimate.

Leonora Investment Co Ltd v Mott Macdonald Ltd (2008)

The leases provided for the tenant to make payments on account based on the landlord's estimate of the anticipated service charge for the forthcoming year and for the landlord to prepare a statement of the actual costs at the end of each service charge year. The tenant was to be credited with the amount of any overpayment whilst in the event of a deficit this would be demanded from the tenant.

The landlord issued statements which indicated the landlord had spent less than the originally estimated amounts and appropriate credit notes were sent to the tenant in respect of the overpayments. However, shortly after issuing the statements the landlord discovered that it had erroneously omitted an item of expenditure and wrote to the tenant requesting an additional payment.

The landlord contended that the tenant was liable to pay any sum being a proportion of actual service costs regardless of when or in what form the landlord demanded payment whilst the tenant submitted its liability depended upon the procedure set down in the lease being followed. The trial judge commented that the obligation to pay sums in advance on a quarterly basis depended upon the landlord exercising the option of preparing an estimate and that if there was no exercise of the option, there was no obligation for the tenant to make payments in advance.

7.2.2 Failure to properly calculate on-account contributions

Failure to calculate tenant's on-account contributions due in accordance with the terms of the lease will render any subsequent demands improper.

Gordon v Selico Co (1986)

A lease required the tenant to pay a maintenance contribution that was to be calculated based upon a computation of the estimated maintenance provision for the year. No such computation was made. It was held that the computation was an essential preliminary to any demand for maintenance contribution and therefore no proper demand had been made.

7.2.3 Estimating on-account payments

A delay in preparing final service charge accounts may not invalidate a demand for future on-account contributions even though a reasonable estimate has not been based on past expenditure.

Peachey Property Corporation Ltd v Henry (1963)

A tenant covenanted to pay a proportionate part of the service charges; the amount to be certified annually as near 6 April as possible.

The tenant also covenanted to pay a quarterly interim sum on account of the annual service charge subject to the proviso that the landlord's agents should certify what was a reasonable interim sum.

The managing agents had last certified a reasonable interim payment in 1959. In 1963, the landlord issued a writ for possession in respect of arrears of one quarter's rent due and the quarterly service charge, which had remained unchanged since 1959. The tenant paid the outstanding rent but contended that she was under no obligation to pay the service charge as the landlord had failed to certify the quarterly on-account sum due.

It was held that the certificate issued in 1959 was valid and that the certificate was not limited in point of time. There was nothing in the clause that determined when the certificate should be given. The final computation of the service charge should have been made on 6 April but the interim payments were not the result of an exact computation.

7.2.4 Misrepresentation

If a landlord misrepresents the amount of service charge payable on a lease, he may lay himself open to an action for damages.

Heinemann v Cooper (1987)

A landlord granted a long lease of a flat at a premium and indicated the service charge would not initially amount to more than £250 per annum.

The first service charge was more than three times this amount and the Court of Appeal held that the purchasers were entitled to damages based upon difference in the value between the flat at a low service charge and the flat with the higher service charge because of the misrepresentation of the vendor landlord when granting the lease.

7.2.5 Reasonableness of estimates

There is no implied obligation that estimates should be reasonable although a tenant may not be liable to pay that proportion of the on-account charges relating to items which are not recoverable under the lease.

Church Commissioners for England v Metroland Ltd (1996)

The tenant of leisure premises situated within the Metro Centre, Gateshead claimed that there was an actual or implied condition to the tenant becoming liable for payment of a provisional service charge that:

(1) a statement of the estimated expenditure has been delivered to the tenant;

(2)   the estimate should relate only to items chargeable under the lease; and

(3)   such estimate should be reasonable.

It was held that: (i) no payment is due until the statement is delivered; and (ii) the statement would be invalid to the extent that items not recoverable from the tenant under the terms of the lease were included. However, the judge rejected the suggestion that the whole statement is a nullity because it contained one item, say, which could not be justified under the relevant lease provisions.

On the question of reasonableness, it was held that business efficacy did not require the implication of such a term. It was only an interim statement and if the landlord unreasonably demanded too much it would, in time, be adjusted. If one allowed it to be reasonable this would lead to disputes, which would impede the cash flow, which was the point of the provision.

7.2.6   Interest on advance payments

There is no implied obligation on the landlord to credit, to the benefit of the service charge, interest earned on advance payments received from tenants.

However, where advance payments are held in separate designated accounts, many landlords do now credit interest earned to the benefit of the service charge account.

Church Commissioners for England v Metroland Ltd (1996)

It was held that there could be no implication into the lease of an obligation for the landlord to credit interest earned to the service charge to give it business efficacy. Interest was specifically mentioned in relation to certain matters such as the sinking fund and the lease also contained a specific term relating to interest on money borrowed. Whilst interest may be earned on money received in advance, landlords may equally incur a deficit as payments are made out. The landlords often deal with this by retaining the rent fund in order to avoid borrowing money and balance the separate accounts.

7.3 INTEREST ON BORROWED FUNDS

7.3.1 Cost of borrowing not recoverable unless lease allows

In the absence of specific provision in the lease, where a landlord finances directly or has to borrow money to finance the provision of the services, the landlord will not be entitled to recover actual or notional interest.

Frobisher (Second Investments) Ltd v Kiloran Trust Co Ltd (1980)

A lease provided for payment in advance of interim sums on account of service charges that were paid into a separate bank account maintained by the landlord's managing agents.

It was held that the interim sums were a service charge to which s. 91A(1)(b) of the *Housing Finance Act* 1972 applied. This provides that a service charge is only recoverable from a tenant once the landlord had defrayed the cost, or at least incurred liability for the cost, of the chargeable item. It therefore followed that the landlord was not entitled to require the interim payments to be made in advance on account of estimated or proposed expenditure.

Deprived of the ability to collect payment in advance, the landlord sought to recover the cost of borrowing money to meet their obligations under the lease.

It was held that the fees payable to the landlord's managing agents were paid for carrying out the general management and administration of the property, which, on the true construction of the leases, could not include interest paid on money borrowed. Nor could a term be implied in the lease as a matter of necessary implication that, in the event of supervening legislation rendering the payment of the service charge in advance unlawful, the tenant was to pay interest. The doctrine of implying a term to give efficacy to an agreement did not apply where there had been a disturbance to the contractual arrangement resulting from statute, then it must be left to the statute to say what is to happen consequentially on its intervention, and that one cannot foist on the parties what some outside body thinks would have been what they would have agreed to in circumstances which neither of them can possibly have contemplated under any circumstances.

Boldmark v Cohen and another (1986)

A tenant was liable to pay a percentage of costs, expenses and outgoings incurred in carrying out maintenance of a block of flats. The lease included for payments of such other sums as the lessor may from time to time expend in respect of the general administration and management of the block. The landlord sought to recover interest on money borrowed in order to carry out maintenance or provide services in accordance with the contractual obligations.

The Court of Appeal held that, although in some circumstances, express provision in a lease enabling tenants to be charged interest might be sensible, the lease in this case did not provide for reimbursement of interest by clear and unambiguous words and therefore the lease, on proper construction, was not capable of including interest payments.

7.3.2 Courts will interpret ambiguities in light of the intention of the parties

Where it appears that the intention of the lease is to give the landlord the ability to charge interest but the wording of the lease is defective, the courts will rectify the lease or so interpret it as to make sense of what is apparently intended.

Skilleter v Charles (1992)

The Court held that the landlord was able to recover interest on borrowed money. Notwithstanding that some words had been omitted in the relevant clause, the plain intention was that interest should be chargeable and to give effect to the intention it was only necessary to insert the obviously missing words or that the same could be achieved by implying a term that interest should be payable in order to give business efficacy to the terms of the lease.

8
Apportionment of the service charge

8.1 TENANT PROPORTIONS DO NOT HAVE TO ADD UP TO 100 PER CENT

There is no general rule that all tenants should be treated in a consistent manner or that the sum of the various individual tenant apportionments should add up to 100 per cent. The way in which a landlord recovers the service charges from tenants will depend upon the specific wording of individual leases and the method of apportionment may differ from lease to lease.

The landlord should bear any shortfall in recovery if the aggregate apportionments are less than 100 per cent. Whilst there is nothing to prevent landlords granting leases where the aggregate apportionments add up to more than 100 per cent, this is arguably immoral as the landlord, in accordance with established principles, should not seek to profit from the provision of services.

However, the way in which the accounts are prepared, as this will relate to the building as a whole, should be consistent.

Mylles v Hall (1980)

A basement flat previously occupied by a resident caretaker, who subsequently left and was not replaced, was then sold off on a long lease. The tenants' contributions to the cost of maintenance was fixed in the lease at $\frac{1}{11}$ and it was held there was no legal obligation on the landlord to reduce the contribution even though the total of the fixed percentages added up to 100 per cent without the caretaker's flat (although the landlord did in fact offer to reduce the tenants' proportion to $\frac{1}{12}$ to recognise what was fair).

Stapel and others v Bellshore Property Investments Ltd (2001)

A building comprised of nine flats on the first to fourth floors above commercial premises. The building had originally been two separate building with frontages on to separate streets.

The leases in respect of flats 1 to 4 and 6 contained a provision for the tenants to pay a proportion of the repair and other costs of 'the building'. The proportion was fixed at ⅙ for four of the flats, and ¼ for the fifth, totalling 91.67 per cent. Flat 5 did not have an equivalent service charge obligation.

It was held that 'the building' meant only that part of the building containing flats 1 to 6. It was apparent that that the fixed percentages were a proper proportion of the costs relating to that part of the building containing only flats 1 to 6 and there would be an obvious disproportion in the service charge provisions if the cost were to relate to the whole building (i.e. including flats 7 to 9). Much clearer wording would have been required for the landlord to sustain that the tenants were to pay a proportion of the costs of the whole building.

8.2 FAIR AND REASONABLE PROPORTIONS

8.2.1 Full recovery of landlord's costs

It is very often the case that modern leases will specify that the tenant is to pay a fair and reasonable proportion of the service charge as determined by the landlord's surveyor. Such determination is often stated as being final and binding.

This basis has the benefit of providing flexibility and, for the landlord, full recovery. The landlord would usually be free to adopt any methods of apportioning the service charge.

Tenants should avoid giving the landlord's surveyor such wide discretion as arguably the basis of apportionment, and thence the tenant's liability, might change from year to year with hardly any justification. This is potentially likely if the ownership is transferred and a new landlord/managing agent recalculates the service charge.

Therefore, unless coupled with a statement as to the basis on which the tenants' apportionment is to be calculated (e.g. floor area, formula, etc.) uncertainty and disputes can often arise.

Campden Hill Towers Ltd v Marshall (1965)

The landlord sought a declaration that the expression 'the premises' meant the aggregate of the premises Gate Hill Court, comprising 30 flats, and Campden Hill Towers, comprising 110 flats.

The landlord also sought a declaration that the clause in the under-lease which imposed an obligation of the tenant to pay a share of $\frac{1}{140}$ of the costs in respect of expenditure, outgoings and other matters should be construed as referring to the aggregate expenditure in respect of Gate Hill Court and Campden Hill Towers.

The tenant's case was that it was not fair to share the aggregate of the costs as rents, rateable values and floor areas of the flats at Campden Hill Towers were substantially higher than those of Gate Hill Court.

It was held that it was the intention of the landlord to aggregate the costs because the share, which the tenant was to meet, was $\frac{1}{140}$. The word 'premises' as used in the context of the lease referred to the whole of the two blocks.

Scottish Mutual Assurance plc v Jardine Public Relations Ltd (1999)

The tenant occupied part of the second floor of an office block under a three-year lease. The landlord carried out only short-term repairs to the roof, intended to deal with immediate leakage problems. The landlord then carried out more extensive repair work and sought recovery of a proportion of the costs from the tenant.

The Court ruled that the tenant was only liable to pay a proportion of the service charge demanded. Whilst accepted as repairs and not improvements, the landlord was only entitled to recover the costs of complying with its repairing obligation over the period of the lease, not the cost of works carried out in performance of the landlord's obligations over a longer term. The fact that the lease was close to expiry was a contributing factor but this does not give tenants the authority that, as a general rule, they cannot be required to pay higher service charge for works carried out towards the end of the term. If a landlord can demonstrate that repairs are necessary to comply with its obligations under the terms of the lease and within the life of the lease, the costs are likely to be recoverable even from a tenant whose lease is about to end.

8.2.2 Challenging the method of calculation

If a lease contains a preamble setting out the landlord's general policy and basis of apportioning the cost of services it will be difficult for either party to challenge the normal construction of the document where this would be contrary to the general statement of intent set out.

Church Commissioners for England v Metroland Ltd (1996)

The tenant of an indoor leisure centre within a large shopping centre claimed his service charge should be limited to the services provided exclusively for his premises. The lease contained a preamble that the landlord had given an undertaking to retail tenants to ensure the leisure tenants made a contribution to the upkeep of common parts and also that the leisure tenants would be subject to a 'weighting' to reflect any exceptional demands made on the services and facilities by the leisure users.

It was held that the purpose of the preamble was to give effect to the obligation which the landlord undertook towards the retail tenants and that therefore the landlord had the power to 'reasonably determine' the service charge chargeable to the leisure tenant to include a proportion of the cost of maintaining and repairing common areas.

8.3 RATEABLE VALUE

Part V of the *Local Government, Planning and Land Act* 1980 abolished the statutory requirement for revision of rateable values for residential properties. Rateable value apportionments for residential properties are therefore becoming increasingly rare due to the lack of a regular revaluation.

Rateable value apportionments are administratively complex as, unless the lease provides to the contrary, the tenants' service charge apportionments would need to be checked against the rating list and recalculated as appropriate every time an invoice was paid.

Moorcroft Estates Ltd v Doxford and another (1980)

A tenant's lease provided that his share of the service charge was to be a 'due proportion' of the costs based on the ratio of the rateable value of the demised premises to the total rateable value of the building. The issue was whether 'rateable value' meant the rateable values at the date of the lease, so that the proportion would then be fixed once and for all, or the rateable value from time to time of the premises demised and the total rateable value from time to time of all parts of the building. It was held that the latter was the correct construction and that the tenant's share of the costs should be based upon the rateable values existent at the time or times when each item of expense was paid.

Universities Superannuation Scheme Ltd v Marks and Spencer plc (1998)

A 150-year lease of a large store in a shopping centre contained provision for payment of a service charge to be certified by the landlord annually. The tenant's proportion of the service charge expenditure was to be calculated by reference to the rateable value of the premises as a proportion of the aggregate of the rateable values of the centre. The landlord's agents incorrectly calculated the amount payable for two years and the landlord sought recovery of the underpayment for both periods. On appeal it was held that the tenant was liable to pay the service charge as the lease referred to the proportion as being that calculated by rateable value. It did not specify the tenant's liability was limited only to that which was certified and payment of an incorrectly calculated sum was not performance of the tenant's obligation.

In this instance, the certification process identified the total service charge expenditure for the centre and not the individual tenant proportions. The service charge was not expressly or by implication final and binding and the landlord was allowed to reopen the service charge calculation.

8.4 FIXED PERCENTAGES

Where fixed percentages are used, the proportions in each lease individually, as compared with the entire structure, will determine the extent to which costs are to be apportioned to tenants.

Campden Hill Towers Ltd v Marshall (1965)

The landlord sought a declaration that the expression 'the premises' meant the aggregate of the premises Gate Hill Court, comprising 30 flats, and Campden Hill Towers, comprising 110 flats.

The landlord also sought a declaration that the clause in the under-lease which imposed an obligation on the tenant to pay a share of $\frac{1}{140}$ of the costs in respect of expenditure, outgoings and other matters should be construed as referring to the aggregate expenditure in respect of Gate Hill Court and Campden Hill Towers.

The tenant's case was that it was not fair to share the aggregate of the costs as rents, rateable values and floor areas of the flats at Campden Hill Towers were substantially higher than those of Gate Hill Court.

It was held that it was the intention of the landlord to aggregate the costs because the share, which the tenant was to meet, was $\frac{1}{140}$. The word 'premises', as used in the context of the lease, referred to the whole of the two blocks.

Adelphi (Estates) v Christie (1984)

A tenant holding a 125-year lease of a flat in a block of flats covenanted to pay to the lessor each year 2.9 per cent of the amount spent by the lessor, as certified by their managing agents, on maintenance of the building.

The lease provided that the lessor should include 'the person or persons for the time being entitled to the reversion immediately expectant on the determination of the term hereby granted'.

In 1980 a concurrent lease of the flat was granted to Adelphi Estates. In 1981 the head-lessor incurred expenditure in maintaining the building of £25,433 and issued a demand to Adelphi for 2.9 per cent of the total cost (£738). Adelphi sought reimbursement of the £738 paid from the tenant.

The tenant denied responsibility for the whole amount contending that as Adelphi were the lessor, they were only liable to pay 2.9 per cent of £738 and not of £25,433.

Dismissing an appeal by the tenant of the earlier county court decision it was held that the definition of 'the lessor' did not provide that the title should apply to no one else and that the word 'lessors' was inappropriate to a person entitled to the reversion of a single flat as opposed to one entitled to the reversion of the whole block. The measure of the contribution to be paid by the tenant must be 2.9 per cent of the head-lessor's expenditure.

The lease clearly indicated that the intention of the parties was that the tenant shall pay 2.9 per cent of the cost of running the whole building and there was nothing in the words used to prevent the court from giving effect to this intention.

Billson v Tristrem (2000)

A tenant of a basement flat of a property divided into five flats covenanted to pay 20 per cent of the proportion of the costs of maintaining entrances, passages, landings and staircases 'enjoyed or used by the lessee in common'. The tenant was held to be liable for payment of a proportion of the costs of maintaining the main entrance even though access to the basement flat was by way of separate entrance and the tenant did not have the right to use the main entrance. In this case, whilst the wording of the lease was inappropriate, it was no coincidence that the percentage was specified as 20 per cent per flat.

Stapel and others v Bellshore Property Investments Ltd (2001)

A building comprised of nine flats on the first to fourth floors above commercial premises. The building had originally been two separate building with frontages on to separate streets.

The leases in respect of flats 1 to 4 and 6 contained a provision for the tenants to pay a proportion of the repair and other costs of 'the building'. The proportion was fixed as ⅙ for four of the flats, and ¼ for the fifth, totalling 91.67 per cent. Flat 5 did not have an equivalent service charge obligation.

It was held that 'the building' meant only that part of the building containing flats 1 to 6. It was apparent that that the fixed percentages were a proper proportion of the costs relating to that part of the building containing only flats 1 to 6 and there would be an obvious disproportion in the service charge provisions if the cost were to relate to the whole building (i.e. including flats 7 to 9). Much clearer wording would have been required for the landlord to sustain that the tenants were to pay a proportion of the costs of the whole building.

8.5 VARYING FIXED PERCENTAGES

8.5.1 Varying fixed percentages where the lease makes provision

Where a lease states that a tenant's proportion of the service charge is to be a fixed percentage, the lease will often allow for the landlord to vary the fixed percentage in the event that the building is altered or circumstances change so that the fixed percentage becomes unfair or unreasonable.

Southend United Football Club Ltd v Denby (1997)

A landlord intended to dispose of 84 flats in five blocks by uniformly worded 199-year leases containing provision for payment of a service charge based on a percentage cost determined by the number of bedrooms. The landlord agreed to bear the proportion attributed to any unlet flats.

The uniform lease contained provision for the landlord to recalculate the percentage if in the opinion of the lessor it became:

'... necessary or desirable to do so by reason of any of the premises in the Estate ceasing to exist or to be habitable or being compulsorily acquired ... or in the number being increased or for any other reason.'

The lease set down a procedure for notifying the lessees and also provided that:

'... in such case as from the date of such event the new percentage shall be substituted for that [shown in the lease].'

In the course of disposing of the flats individually, the landlord sold one of the blocks containing 24 flats to a housing association on a 999-year lease. It subsequently became apparent that the provisions of the housing association lease did not permit the landlord to recover in full the amount they would have if the flats had been let separately, resulting in a 26.5 per cent shortfall. The landlord therefore served notice to tenants to increase their percentages, backdated to the commencement of the housing association lease.

The tenants argued that the landlord's action in selling the block did not constitute a relevant reason for amending the service charge percentages or if it did, the landlord could not backdate the operation of the notice.

The leases contained various provisions to the effect that the landlord should be able to recover the service charge costs in full. It was held that the consequence of accepting the arguments put forward by the tenants would be to restrict the landlord to disposing of unsold flats by only one method. The landlord's notice was therefore valid and the expression 'the date of such event' referred to the causative event (the disposal date) rather than the date of notification to tenants.

8.5.2 Varying fixed percentages where the lease makes no provision

If the lease makes no provision for future variation of the percentage should the building be altered or circumstances change, there is no obligation on the landlord to amend the tenant's contributions even if the result would be to allow the landlord to recover more than 100 per cent of the total expenditure.

Mylles v Hall (1980)

A basement flat in a block of 12 flats, previously occupied by a resident caretaker, who subsequently left and was not replaced, was then sold off on a long lease. The tenants' contributions to the cost of maintenance was fixed in the lease at $1/11$ and it was held there was no legal obligation on the landlord to reduce the contribution even though the total of the fixed percentages added up to 100 per cent without the caretakers flat (although the landlord did offer to reduce the tenants' proportion to $1/12$ to recognise what was fair).

8.5.3 Intervention by the courts

Where leases are granted with fixed percentages and circumstances change to make the fixed percentages unfair or inequitable, the courts may intervene and decide on an alternative fair method of apportioning the service charge.

Pole Properties Ltd v Feinberg (1981)

A tenant's lease provided that he should contribute $2/7$ (based on floor area) of costs of providing heating to the demised premises. The building was joined with neighbouring premises and the heating system extended to include internal passages and common parts. The landlord sought to apply the $2/7$ calculation under the new conditions. It was held that there had been a radical change and that the Court had to do what was fair and reasonable in the circumstances and altered the lease so that a directly heated volume basis of calculation should be applied.

Broomleigh Housing Association v Hughes (1999)

A tenant in a block of flats covenanted to contribute proportionately to the service charge.

The landlord covenanted to keep the property in good repair. The landlord replaced windows in other flats, but not those in the tenant's flat as these had been recently replaced at the tenant's own expense.

Notwithstanding that the replacement of the windows in the tenant's flat did not constitute a breach of covenant as the landlord had subsequently given the requisite consent, it was held that this did not reduce or vary the obligation upon the tenant to contribute to the total service charge. There was no provision in the lease to allow for this to happen.

Furthermore, the fact that the landlord might have waived the obligation to contribute for some tenants, that is to say those who had obtained a prior written consent, does not create any right or expectation that other tenants should be treated in the same way provided the waiver did not increase the liability of other tenants and any loss arising from such a waiver falls upon the landlord.

8.6 INDEX LINKED SERVICES CHARGES

8.6.1 Changes to stated indexes

Where a lease specifies a formula for increasing the service charge payable in accordance with a particular index, a common-sense approach is taken to continue using the stated index even though it may change and be calculated on a slightly different basis.

Cumshaw v Bowen (1987)

A lease provided for a tenant's service charge to be £100 per annum plus £1 per annum for each point or part of a point by which the Retail Prices Index rose above a figure of 110.4, but if the index should cease to be published or be made available, the increase in the service charge was to be based upon the increase in the landlord's costs to be determined by an independent surveyor.

Following changes to the commodities and services included within the index, weightings and the bases, used in calculating the Retail Prices Index, the direction in the lease about the additional £1 per annum for each rise in point in the index could not be literally applied.

It was held that the revised index remained the index to which the lease referred and that it had neither ceased to be published nor ceased to be available. Changes in the basket of commodities and items used and their weightings, reflected changes in habits and tastes and a simple mathematical formula could be used to convert the new figures to increases on the old base.

8.6.2 Tenant's liability may not automatically increase in line with index

A service charge that limits any increases in the cost recoverable by the landlord to an index, does not necessarily imply that the tenants' liability automatically increases when the actual costs rise (or fall) to a lesser rate.

Jollybird Ltd v Fairzone Ltd (1990)

The landlord covenanted to repair and maintain a central heating system. The tenants covenanted to pay a fair proportion of the expenses incurred, calculated by reference to floor area, such charge being not less than a fixed rate per square foot and which could be 'increased proportionately at any time … if the cost of fuel … shall at any time exceed the cost thereof at the date of the lease'.

The landlord sought to increase the rate per square foot stated in the lease based on the percentage increase in fuel costs which would have resulted in the landlord making a profit from the supply of heating. It was held that the landlord was only entitled to make a charge calculated by reference to floor area, subject to the minimum charge set out in the lease. Although a profit might arise where fuel costs were below the minimum charge, the proviso could not be construed as intending to give the landlord a profit in other circumstances.

8.7 CONCESSIONS

The owner should meet the cost of any special concession given by an owner to any one occupier.

Broomleigh Housing Association v Hughes (1999)

A tenant in a block of flats covenanted to contribute proportionately to the service charge.

The landlord covenanted to keep the property in good repair. The landlord replaced windows in other flats, but not those in the tenant's flat as these had been recently replaced at the tenant's own expense.

Notwithstanding that the replacement of the windows in the tenant's flat did not constitute a breach of covenant as the landlord has subsequently given the requisite consent, it was held that this did not reduce or vary the obligation upon the tenant to contribute to the total service charge. There was no provision in the lease to allow for this to happen.

Furthermore, the fact that the landlord might have waived the obligation to contribute for some tenants, that is to say those who had obtained a prior written consent, does not create any right or expectation that other tenants should be treated in the same way provided the waiver did not increase the liability of other tenants and any loss arising from such a waiver falls upon the landlord.

9
Certification of service charge accounts

A service charge will often provide for certification of the actual costs incurred by the landlord's surveyor. Where statutory regulation imposes obligations upon the landlord of residential property, this is usually to be viewed as being in addition to, and not instead of, any specific requirements or obligations set down under the lease.

CLRA 2002 introduced an amended s. 21 of LTA 1985 which obliges the landlord to provide residential tenants with regular statements of expenditure based on the following rules:

(1) Each accounting period must not be more than 12 months.

(2) Each statement must specify:

 (a) the total service cost for the relevant period;

 (b) the service charge payable by the tenant and by other tenants who contribute to the service costs;

 (c) any service charge sums in hand at the beginning of the accounting period;

 (d) any service charge sums to remain in hand at the end of the accounting period; and

 (e) any related matters and any further matters prescribed by regulations.

(3) The landlord must also supply:

 (a) a certificate certified by a qualified accountant, who must be independent of the landlord, as satisfying the requirements and being a fair summary and properly supported;

      (b) a summary of the rights and obligations of tenants of dwellings in relation to service charges.

    (4) The statement must be issued within six months of the end of the relevant accounting period.

Failure to comply with these requirements may result in the tenant being entitled to withhold payment of service charges.

9.1 CONCLUSIVENESS, FINAL AND BINDING

9.1.1 Purpose of certification

The purpose of the annual certificate is to certify the annual expenditure and not to state the amount payable by the tenant.

Universities Superannuation Scheme Ltd v Marks and Spencer plc (1998)

A 150-year lease of a large store in a shopping centre contained provision for payment of a service charge to be certified annually by the landlord. The tenant's proportion of the service charge expenditure was to be calculated by reference to the rateable value of the premises as a proportion of the aggregate of the rateable values of the centre. The landlord's agents incorrectly calculated the amount payable for two years and the landlord sought recovery of the underpayment for both periods. On appeal, it was held that the tenant was liable to pay the service charge as the lease referred to the proportion as being that calculated by rateable value. It did not specify that the tenant's liability was limited only to that which was certified and payment of an incorrectly calculated sum was not performance of the tenant's obligation.

In this instance, the certification process identified the total service charge expenditure for the centre and not the individual tenant proportions. The service charge was not expressly or by implication final and binding and the landlord was allowed to reopen the service charge calculation.

9.1.2 Certification as a condition precedent

The issue of a certificate may be a condition precedent to the tenant's liability and failure to issue a certificate, or if a certificate is issued in error, may absolve tenants from liability for payment of any of the service charge.

Finchbourne v Rodrigues (1976)

The amount of tenant's contribution was to be 'ascertained and certified by the lessor's managing agents acting as experts and not as arbitrators'. The issue of a valid certificate was held to be a condition precedent to the recovery of the service charge. The lessor was subsequently discovered to be the managing agents themselves. The agents' certificate was held to be invalid and 'managing agents must, according to the terms of the lease, be somebody different from the lessor'.

CIN Properties Ltd v Barclays Bank plc (1986)

An agreement obliged the tenant to pay a proportion of the costs of repairs subject to the proviso that the landlord would not accept any estimates or place orders for work without first submitting them to the tenant for approval. The landlord placed orders for the carrying out of extensive works without consulting the tenant. The Court of Appeal held that the proviso was an unequivocal condition precedent to the tenant's liability.

9.1.3 Final and binding

The service charge clause will frequently provide that the landlord's certificate of expenditure is to be final and binding. However, a certificate purporting to be conclusive on a point of law is invalid as this is viewed as an attempt to supplant the jurisdiction of the courts to decide on such matters. A certificate can therefore amount to conclusive evidence that the amounts thereby certified are correct but cannot preclude the tenant's right to seek assistance from the courts in determining disputes.

Davstone Estate's Lease, Re, Manprop v O'Dell (1969)

Service charge expenditure was subject to certification by the landlord's surveyor, such certificate to be 'final and binding and not subject to challenge in any manner'. It was held that the wording of the lease was contrary to public policy in purporting to oust the jurisdiction of the courts on questions of law.

Rapid Results College v Angell (1986)

Tenants of premises comprising the second (and top) floor of a building were required to contribute towards repair works; such contribution to be demanded by a certificate signed by the landlord's surveyor whose decision was stated to be binding on the parties. The parapet of the building had to be rebuilt after the bricks became saturated with damp. The claim was based mainly on an item, 'maintenance of the exterior', in a list of items of expenditure.

It was held that the landlord's surveyor's certificate was not conclusive as to whether items listed in the certificate did, as a matter of law, fall within the particular provision in the lease.

9.1.4 Manifest error

Many modern leases of commercial property provide for the service charge statement to be conclusive and binding on the parties as to matters of fact save for manifest error. This does not, however, mean that any error which might subsequently be uncovered would nullify the conclusive and binding nature of the statement provided.

Church Commissioners for England v Metroland Ltd (1996)

If a statement contains a certificate as prescribed under the lease, it is conclusive and liability follows. It is conclusive, save only for manifest errors and as to matters of law, which would include whether or not an item of expenditure is recoverable from the tenant under the provisions of the lease; the manifest error must appear on the face of the certificate. The protection for the tenant lies in the ability (if provided for under the terms of the lease) to inspect the vouchers to determine whether any errors of law may exist. But the tenant cannot go behind the certificate on matters of fact.

9.1.5 Error in 'final and binding' certificate

If a certificate is 'final and binding' (with no manifest error proviso) and is subsequently found to be in error, the amount certified will not be recoverable. However, due to the 'final' nature of the certificate, the landlord may not then be able to issue another certificate and therefore find he is unable to recover any monies at all.

Many modern leases provide for the certificate to be final and binding 'except in the case of manifest error' to avoid the situation where the landlord is prevented from reissuing a corrected and valid certificate.

Rapid Results College Ltd v Angell (1986)

Tenants were required to contribute towards repair works; such contribution to be demanded by a certificate signed by the landlord's surveyor whose decision was stated to be final and binding on the parties.

It was common ground that the landlord's surveyor's certificate was not conclusive as to whether items listed in the certificate did as a matter of law fall within the particular provision in the lease. By virtue of the certificate being 'final' the landlord may be precluded from issuing another subsequently corrected certificate and therefore from recovering any money at all.

9.1.6 Misinterpretation of the lease provisions

A certificate may not be binding if the surveyor or accountant who has provided the certificate has misinterpreted the lease provisions.

Barrington v Sloane Properties Ltd (2007)

The landlord of a block of flats contracted to carry out substantial building works over a three-year period. The lease provided for the tenant to pay 24.24 per cent of the 'actual cost' to the landlord of providing the services and for such sum to be certified annually by the landlord's accountant, such certificate to be conclusive.

The works contract was supervised by an architect who valued the work from time to time and issued certificates for payment. Each certificate was subject to a 5 per cent retention and the balance was payable within 14 days of the certificate.

The landlord's accountant certified the service charge for each year based on the estimated value of the works carried out rather than the amount which had actually been charged and become payable in each service charge year.

The Lands Tribunal held that 'actual cost' was limited to sums that had fallen for payment in each year and did not include the cost of works undertaken but not yet payable. As to the conclusive nature of the certificate, the Tribunal held that the accountant acted on the wrong meaning of 'actual cost' and therefore the certificates were not binding.

9.1.7 Reopening of previous years' service charge accounts

Where the lease provides no reference, either express or by implication, that the certificate should be final and conclusive, the landlord may be able to reopen service charge accounts for previous years if an error is subsequently found which requires that the tenants' service charges payments be recalculated.

Universities Superannuation Scheme Ltd v Marks and Spencer plc (1998)

A 150-year lease of a large store in a shopping centre contained provision for payment of a service charge to be certified annually by the landlord. The tenant's proportion of the service charge expenditure was to be calculated by reference to the rateable value of the premises as a proportion of the aggregate of the rateable values of the centre. The landlord's agents incorrectly calculated the amount payable for two years and the landlord sought recovery of the underpayment for both periods. The Court of Appeal held that the tenant was liable to pay the service charge as the lease referred to the proportion as being that calculated by rateable value. It did not specify the tenant's liability was limited only to that which was certified and payment of an incorrectly calculated sum was not performance of the tenant's obligation.

In this instance, the certification process identified the total service charge expenditure for the centre and not the individual tenant proportions. The service charge was not expressly, or by implication, final and binding and the landlord was allowed to reopen the service charge calculation.

Leonora Investment Co Ltd v Mott Macdonald Ltd (2008)

The tenant held separate leases of four floors of a 13-storey office block.

The leases provided for the tenant to make payments on account based on the landlord's estimate of the anticipated service charge for the forthcoming year and for the landlord to prepare a statement of the actual costs at the end of each service charge year. The tenant was to be credited with the amount of any overpayment whilst in the event of a deficit this would be demanded from the tenant.

The landlord issued statements which indicated the landlord had spent less than the originally estimated amounts and appropriate credit notes were sent to the tenant in respect of the overpayments. However, shortly after issuing the statements the landlord discovered that it had erroneously omitted an item of expenditure and wrote to the tenant requesting an additional payment of some £260,000.

It was held that the tenant was not liable to pay the further invoice raised by the landlord as this did not follow the procedure set down in the lease. However, the Court did not construe the lease as limiting the landlord to one balancing charge in each year although to be valid the new demand should have included a revised statement of total service charge costs for the service charge period in question.

9.1.8 Certification by independent expert

Certification by an independent expert, who makes a decision on a question of law, has been held not to be invalid as supplanting the jurisdiction of the court.

Jones v Sherwood Computer Services plc (1992)

This case concerned an agreement to purchase shares for consideration related to the amount of sales. The accountants were to determine the amount of sales acting as experts, such determination to be conclusive, final and binding for all purposes. The accountants, without giving reasons, determined an amount that was subsequently challenged on the basis that it had not taken into account transactions that ought to have been taken into account.

The Court of Appeal held that the parties had agreed to be bound by the report of an expert and that the report could not be challenged in the courts on the ground that mistakes had been made in its preparation unless it could be shown that the expert had departed from the instructions given in a material respect. The accountants had done precisely what they had been asked to do and there was no question of bad faith. Their determination was not therefore subject to challenge.

Nikko Hotels (UK) Ltd v MEPC plc (1991)

This case concerned a somewhat unusual rent review provision in the lease of a hotel where the increase in rent was to be geared to the increases in the charges made for accommodation to customers of the hotel. The lease contained provision for the production of certified statements of average room rates at the relevant review date. The dispute arose from the tenants' calculation of using room rates actually achieved during the year whereas the landlord contended that the calculation should be based on the published room prices actually available.

The dispute, although a question of construction, was referred to a chartered accountant appointed as an expert, who found in favour of the landlord.

The Court upheld the principles established in the unreported case of *Jones v Sherwood Computer Services plc* in that if parties agree to refer to the final and conclusive judgment of an expert an issue which involves the solution of a question of construction, the expert's decision will be final and conclusive, and therefore not open to challenge on the ground that the expert's decision in construction was erroneous in law, unless it could be shown that the expert had not performed the task assigned to him. If the expert answered the right question in the wrong way, his decision will nevertheless be binding. If he has answered the wrong question, his decision will be a nullity.

9.2 FORM OF CERTIFICATION

In respect of commercial property, there is no legislative guidance as to the form in which the certificate should be provided. The form of the 'certificate' needs to be clear in its intent. In order to amount to a certificate of expenditure, the words 'I certify' are not required if, in all other matters, the documentation issued by the landlord or the managing agents complies with the intent of the service charge provision of the lease.

Wagon Finance Ltd v Demelt Holdings Ltd (1997)

Under the terms of a lease of commercial property, the tenant was liable to pay a service charge, the amount of which was to be ascertained and certified annually by a certificate 'signed by the landlord or its Agent or Professional Auditors (at the Landlords discretion)'.

The certificate was required to:

' ... contain a fair summary of the Landlord's Liabilities in respect of the Service during the Landlord's accounting period ... [which] ... shall be conclusive evidence for the purposes hereof ...'

The landlord carried out refurbishment and improvement works to the common parts in respect of which the tenant was liable under the service charge.

It was held that certification of the expenditure incurred was a condition precedent which must be complied with by the landlord before the landlord could claim under the lease for the payment of a service charge by the tenant. The relevant document was signed by the landlord and contained a fair summary of the work done and it furnished a final account. However, although the words 'I certify' were not used, the documents issued by the landlord were held to be an unequivocal statement of the liability of the tenant, the 'certificate' was adequate and accordingly the landlord was entitled to claim the relevant money from the tenant.

9.3 TIME LIMITS

Landlord and Tenant Act 1985

Section 20B of LTA 1985 states that, in respect of residential dwellings, a tenant shall not be liable for payment of any costs incurred more than 18 months before a demand for payment of the service charge is served on the tenant unless, within the period, the tenant has been notified in writing that the costs had been incurred and that the tenant would be required to contribute to them by way of the service charge.

Commonhold and Leasehold Reform Act 2002

Section 21 of CLRA 2002 (see above) also now requires certificates and accounts to be issued within six months of the end of the relevant accounting period.

Commercial leases will often provide for the landlord to certify the service charge expenditure within a specified time limit following the end of the service charge period.

9.3.1 Failure to serve notice within time may not exempt tenants from liability

The failure to serve notice does not exempt the tenant from liability for payment of the service charge if the tenant has made interim on-account payments and the total expenditure is less than the interim service charge demanded.

Gilje v Charlegrove Securities Ltd (No 2) (2003)

Tenants of a block of flats covenanted to quarterly interim payments in advance of anticipated expenditure and the payment of a balancing charge at the end of the service charge period. The actual amounts expended were less than the interim quarterly payments demanded but the landlord did not supply the accounts of actual expenditure within the time limits set down under s. 20B of LTA 1985. The tenants claimed the landlord was not entitled to recover any of the expenditure incurred more than 18 months previously.

It was held that s. 20B did not apply where: (i) payments on account are made; (ii) the actual expenditure does not exceed the payments made on account; and (iii) no request by the lessor for any further payment by the tenant needs to be, or is in fact, made.

9.3.2 Notice under s. 20B must be in respect of costs incurred and not costs that are uncertain or to be incurred

A tenant cannot be considered to have been notified of a liability for actual costs if the landlord has failed to identify costs which had been incurred. In such circumstances the landlord will be unable to recover costs in excess of the maximum amounts prescribed by statute.

London Borough of Islington v Abdel-Malek (2006)

The tenant occupied a flat in one of four adjoining blocks owned by Islington Council.

The landlord sought estimates for various works including repairs, enhancements and window repairs, the lowest tender for which was in the sum of £556,000. The landlord gave notification of the estimates received and the likely contribution payable but did provide full copies of the estimates but only a summary of the lowest one.

After commencement of the works but prior to completion, the Council issued an estimated invoice for the tenant's contribution and gave no information about the costs actually incurred to date.

The Tribunal held that s. 20B of LTA 1985 prevents a landlord recovering costs if, within 18 months of incurring the costs, it has not issued an invoice or notified the tenant that the costs have been incurred and will be invoiced.

A notice under s. 20B had to be in respect of costs incurred and not costs that were uncertain or to be incurred. The landlord could not therefore show it had notified the tenant of a liability for actual costs and consequently could not recover the sums claimed.

9.3.3 Time of the essence

In respect of commercial property, unless the lease states that time is to be of the essence, such wording is regarded as being similar to rent reviews and that the time limits set down in the lease have no effect.

West Central Investments v Borovik (1977)

The landlord of a block of flats was obliged to arrange for the preparation and audit of accounts relating to the costs, charges, etc. incurred in providing services and to serve notice within two months of the financial year end. The landlord failed to certify the expenditure incurred for four years. The tenant claimed they were not liable, as the landlord had failed to prepare accounts and serve notices. It was held that time was not of the essence and the lessees were liable.

9.3.4 Importing time of the essence

Where no reference is made in the lease to time being of the essence, a tenant may be able to impute this by service of notice upon the landlord to issue a certificate. If the landlord fails to produce a certificate within a reasonable period given in the tenant's notice, the landlord may lose the right to recover any balancing charges due.

Barclays Bank plc v Savile Estates Ltd (2002)

This involved a rent review where a tenant served notice upon his landlord giving 28 days to implement a review, which had been due some years previously. The landlord ignored the tenant's request and the Court of Appeal held that the landlord had lost his right to implement the review and that time can be made of the essence by reasonable notice.

9.4 IDENTITY OF THE CERTIFIER

Leases will usually state that the certifier must be the landlord's surveyor or accountant, often with a description of the credentials/qualifications required in order for somebody to qualify as certifier of the service charge under the terms of the lease. In certain circumstances, the clause might state that the surveyor or accountant may be an employee of the landlord.

9.4.1 Certifier must be independent of the landlord

In the absence of any qualifying wording, the surveyor or accountant must be someone independent of the landlord.

Finchbourne v Rodrigues (1976)

The amount of tenant's contribution was to be 'ascertained and certified by the lessor's managing agents acting as experts and not as arbitrators'. The issue of a valid certificate was held to be a condition precedent to the recovery of the service charge. The lessor was subsequently discovered to be the managing agents themselves. The agents' certificate was held to be invalid and 'managing agents must, according to the terms of the lease, be somebody different from the lessor'.

9.4.2 Landlord's surveyor and managing agent must be different

Where the lease provides for any dispute to be determined by the 'landlord's surveyor', the certifier is acting in an arbitral role between the landlord and the tenants. Somebody therefore acting in the capacity of a managing agent *and* surveyor cannot function as an arbiter. This would also be true if the person issuing the certificate turns out to be the same person as the landlord himself.

However, if the managing company is in the same ownership as the landlord (e.g. a subsidiary) and appropriate management contracts are in place, they will be regarded as separate entities in most cases.

Concorde Graphics v Andromeda Investments SA (1982)

This case concerned an industrial estate where the tenants were liable to contribute to expenses incurred in maintaining and repairing the common parts of the estate. After the appointment of new managing agents, the amount of the service charge contributions demanded increased substantially. The leases contained provision that in case of a 'difference' as to the contribution, the matter was to be settled 'by the landlord's surveyor' whose decision was to be 'final and binding' on the parties.

As the function of deciding a 'difference' as to the amount of tenant's contribution was essentially arbitral, it was held that the landlord's managing agents could not, in their capacity as the landlord's surveyors, make a 'final and binding' decision on such a 'difference'. The landlord would have to appoint other surveyors for that purpose.

9.4.3 Where the lease identifies the certifier as a specific individual the certifier cannot be substituted

St Modwen Developments (Edmonton) Ltd v Tesco Stores Ltd (2007)

St Modwen acquired the freehold reversion to premises in the Edmonton Green shopping centre from the borough council. The landlord brought proceedings to establish its entitlement to: (i) service charges certified by its finance director in place of the borough treasurer; (ii) a contribution to the cost of refuse collection for other tenants, in circumstances where the tenant disposed of its own refuse; and (iii) a 10 per cent management fee.

With regard to the matter of certification, the lease required the service charge to be certified by the council's borough treasurer. The parties to the original lease had not anticipated that the property might be sold and that the person who might be required to be issued a certificate would be other than the borough treasurer. In the absence of the borough treasurer the contractual mechanism provided for by the lease no longer took effect.

The new landlord still had a contractual right to recover a service charge, but, with no contractual mechanism for doing so, it had to bring its claim in a court, subject to the arbitration provisions of the lease.

Index

The *Case in Point* series

The *Case in Point* series is a popular set of concise practical guides to legal issues in land, property and construction. Written for the property professional, they get straight to the key issues in a refreshingly jargon-free style.

Areas covered:

Party Walls
Stock code: 7269
Published: May 2004

Estate Agency
Stock code: 7472
Published: July 2004

Rent Review
Stock code: 8531
Published: May 2005

Expert Witness
Stock code: 8842
Published: August 2005

Lease Renewal
Stock code: 8711
Published: August 2005

VAT in Property and Construction
Stock code: 8840
Published September 2005

Construction Adjudication
Stock code: 9040
Published October 2005

Dilapidations
Stock code: 9113
Published January 2006

Planning Control
Stock code: 9391
Published April 2006

Building Defects
Stock code: 9949
Published July 2006

Contract Administration
Stock code: 16419
Published March 2007

Construction claims
Stock code: 16978
Published December 2007

Easements & Other Rights
Stock code: 17245
Published March 2008

Negligence in Valuation and Surveys (2nd edition)
Stock code: 17550
Published: August 2008

If you would like to be kept informed when new *Case in Point* titles are published, please e-mail **rbmarketing@rics.org.uk**

All RICS Books titles can be ordered direct by:

☎   Telephoning 0870 333 1600 (Option 3)

🖱   Online at www.ricsbooks.com

📠   E-mail mailorder@rics.org.uk